Your Christian Wedding

Your Christian Wedding

Elizabeth Swadley

BROADMAN PRESS · Nashville, Tennessee

4279–02

ISBN: 0-8054-7902-3

DEWEY DECIMAL CLASSIFICATION NUMBER: 395
Library of Congress catalog card number: 66–15149
Printed in the United States of America

Contents

1

What Is a Christian Wedding?

Weddings are meant to be Christian! Marriage is an institution established by God the Father and honored by Jesus his Son. Wouldn't it have been wonderful to have been a guest at the wedding in Cana of Galilee?

The Bible tells us little about Cana, and even less about the wedding there, but God's Word does tell us much about Christ's presence at that wedding. The wedding was Christian because Christ was there. His presence made the difference!

A wedding today is not necessarily Christian because the ceremony is performed in a beautiful sanctuary or because the vows are solemnized by a minister of God or because the music is all "church music." These are all elements of a Christian wedding, but they do not make the wedding *Christian*. To make a wedding Christian, Jesus Christ himself, through the Holy Spirit, must attend and must be in evidence.

I'm thinking of three wonderful weddings:

My grandfather, who was a devout Christian, told me that when the Civil War was over and he was discharged to return home, he rode horseback to the home of his beloved, and said to her, "Paulina, get your horse. We're going to town to be married." She had been waiting for that day, so she needed no coaxing.

They were riding side by side down the country road when

they met the minister coming toward them. Grandpa told him of his desire to marry Paulina, and the minister replied, "Pull your horses close together and join right hands." This they did and the minister said the ceremony. Then he left, promising them he would record the marriage at the town courthouse.

Grandfather and his bride started back home. They had only gone a short distance when this new groom said, "Paulina, dear, don't you think you should give me that kiss you promised me on our wedding day?"

And Grandmother pulled her horse in close, leaned from the saddle and sealed the marriage with the promised kiss.

There was no music except that which rang in their hearts, no flowers except those growing by the wayside, and no *audible* praying. But there were prayers in the hearts of both bride and groom, and they both declared later that Christ was with them all the way.

This marriage lasted more than sixty years and bore nine sons. Two of those sons became ministers. Would you not say that this marriage, though a bit unusual, was thoroughly *Christian?*

The second wonderful wedding I'm thinking about is the wedding of my parents. Theirs was a simple home ceremony. There was no music. There were no flowers. There was no formal attire. But there was prayer and there was a wonderful minister who performed a sweet and sacred ceremony. Christ was in evidence. My father, I am told, beamed and declared, "Amen!" and "Amen!" And my mother says that she was so far up in the clouds that heaven seemed very near.

This " 'til-death-do-us-part" marriage lasted until Daddy was called home to glory almost thirty-six years later. Was the wedding of my parents—without sanctuary and without hymns—Christian? Of course it was!

The third wedding I'm remembering is my own. It was a beautiful church wedding! There were lots of flowers, candles, and attendants in beautiful dresses. I married my pastor's finest son, and the whole congregation was present. There was sweet music, too. In my own eyes everything seemed just right. My daddy said the ceremony and meant every word of it. Every memory of that wonderful day is a happy one.

But all of the outside appearance did not make our wedding Christian. It was Christian because Christ was there, dwelling in the hearts of the people involved.

The horseback wedding on the country road . . . the simple wedding in a home . . . the large wedding in my church . . . *all* were as Christian as that wedding in Cana of Galilee, *because* Christ himself was an honored guest.

I do not mean to disparage the large, church wedding. It's great to see the happy groom take his radiant bride to himself and to proclaim "in the presence of God and these witnesses" that he will love and cherish her "from this day forward, for better for worse, for richer for poorer, in sickness and in health, so long as we both shall live."

But whether your wedding is large or small, elegant or simple, public or private—it can only be *Christian* if the hearts and lives of the people involved have been transformed by the presence of Christ himself. And the transformation must show in your conversation, your acts and deeds, your plans and dreams, from the moment you become engaged until you hear the pronouncement, "Let not man put asunder!"—and for that matter—forever after.

A Christian should have good manners. Jesus laid the foundation for all systems of etiquette when he said, "As ye would that men should do to you, do ye also to them."

That's what this book is all about. I have compiled for you all the etiquette involved in planning a wedding, in order that you may be thoroughly proper—and I have added all I can think of in the field of human relations to help you also be thoroughly Christian.

2

Now You Can Tell It

You're engaged! Your dreams are coming true at last! Suddenly your smile has more sparkle, your step a bit more bounce. Life has become many-splendored. Your heart is bubbling over with joy and you are bursting to tell the world.

That's wonderful. You can *tell* it and *tell* it and *tell* it again. Here's how:

People to Tell First

Your parents!—It will undoubtedly come as no surprise to them. After all, they've been watching you walk about on Cloud Nine; and, whether you realize it or not, they can tell what ticks in your heart and your head during these romantic days. (They've been there themselves, you know.) But even though it will not surprise them, *tell* them anyway. It is your parents who will make arrangements for, pay for, and help plan your wedding. Your relationship with them is changing now from total dependency to mature, independent respect. So give them the privilege of being the first to know officially. It is a lovely way to "honor your father and your mother."

And here's some important phraseology your parents will appreciate. Don't just flatly announce, "Jim and I are going to be

4

married" (even though you know full well that nobody on earth can stop you). Instead say, "Jim and I would like to be married." This is simply good psychology and will let your father enjoy that good, old-fashioned feeling that he is permitting it all—that he is really *giving* you in marriage.

Your minister!—A wedding is a sacred service. If it is to be a church wedding, it will be conducted in a sanctuary that is dedicated to the glory and worship of God. Many churches have established policies covering everything from when you may use the sanctuary, how it may be decorated, who may perform the ceremony, and even what music may be used. This is as it should be, for marriage is a divine institution. Even if your wedding vows are to be solemnized in your own home, your minister will still want to guide your planning. He will provide invaluable counseling concerning the details of your wedding and also in the establishment of your Christian home. He can clarify for you the church policies governing weddings. And he can answer many of your premarital questions, both simple and complex.

One of the most important reasons for consulting a minister early is that you cannot set your wedding date until you have cleared it with him and have established it on the church calendar.

Use the same polite "would-like-to-be" approach that you used with your parents. And tell him soon after you have told your parents. Sometimes the bride and groom visit the minister together and sometimes the bride and her mother make this first visit. Either is proper. The minister will make further appointments for counseling with all concerned before the actual wedding.

Your close friends.—Tell those near you, and to those far away whom you know will welcome the glad news, be courteous enough to drop a note. Now you can joyously say, "Jim and I are going to be married." Engraved engagement announcements are not in good taste, but personal notes definitely are.

The newspaper.—Newspaper announcements vary from city to city and from newspaper to newspaper. You will want to follow the pattern used in your community.

It is your mother's responsibility to notify the society editor and to ask her for procedures to be followed in making the announcement. The society editor will, upon request, mail a questionnaire to be filled out and returned. All newspapers ask for the full name of the bride; her home address and phone number; name of her parents and their address; full name of the groom and his home address; name of his parents and their address; and date the announcement is to be released.

Some newspapers ask for some of the following details: Date and place of planned ceremony; the bride's college and sorority; the groom's college and fraternity; any college honors of either; business affiliation of the groom; and grandparents of both the bride and the groom.

The society editor can also advise you about a picture to be used with the announcement. Usually the picture must be a black and white glossy print and of a specific size. Some newspapers prefer to use pictures made by their own photographers. Others accept commercially made portraits. Some newspapers have a set fee for the printing of the announcement and pictures. Most do not.

Whether your engagement portrait is made by a newspaper photographer or a commercial photographer, you can give a silent but beautiful Christian testimony—simply by the way you look in the picture, by the way you dress, and by the way you smile.

The Engagement Ring

Is it necessary?—No, you can certainly become engaged without wearing a ring. Some couples, for economic reasons, choose to forego the expense of a diamond ring because the money is badly needed elsewhere—perhaps for college tuition. Others prefer simple matching gold bands—the bride's worn without an engagement ring. Occasionally a bride will prefer a single wedding ring set with diamonds rather than two rings. This is a matter of individual choice and is within the realm of good taste.

Is it traditional?—Yes, the tradition of giving a ring to mark an engagement goes back to Europe in the Middle Ages.

The circle is the emblem of eternity and stands for the "foreverness" of your marital relationship.

Gold is a symbol of all that is pure and holy.

An Italian legend proclaims that the diamond itself has been refined in the fires of love and will, therefore, insure happiness in marriage.

Who selects the ring?—The bride may choose the ring by following these simple rules of discretion. First, the bridegroom can visit a jewelry store and choose several sets of rings in a price range within his budget. The jeweler will set these rings aside until the bridegroom returns with his fiancée. The bride then, with the help of the groom and the jeweler, selects the set most pleasing to her taste. She can also select the groom's ring at this time, if he is to be given one. When she has made her selection, she can quietly browse in another part of the store while the groom pays for or makes arrangements to pay for her rings. The bride, of course, pays for the groom's ring.

Sometimes the groom selects the ring, to the surprise and delight of the bride. And it may be even more special to her because he selected it.

After the purchases have been completed, the groom takes the engagement ring along with him, or picks it up after it has been initialed and gives it to his bride-to-be at a romantic moment of his own choosing.

You will not see your wedding ring again until you are standing at the altar.

What about initials?—You may want to have the rings initialed. Your jeweler can advise you about this, but such initialing usually reads, "R. E. C. to L. S. H." Sometimes the date of the engagement or some special word or phrase full of meaning only to you is added. If such is your wish, do not hesitate to have the engraving done. The jeweler is accustomed to such sentiment. There is no reason to be embarrassed about it.

The Announcement Party

You may wish to celebrate your engagement with an announcement party. The announcement party is given by the bride's parents but can take any one of many different forms. It can be a simple morning coffee, to which close friends are invited; or, an afternoon tea, for which few or many invitations are extended. It can be a dinner or an evening social event.

News of the engagement may be proclaimed on favors given to guests as they arrive—miniature wedding bells, miniature cakes, miniature rings—or the news may be told on place cards or napkins.

One clever mother of the bride placed dainty little net rice bags at each place setting for her daughter's engagement party. Each bag was tied with a pretty ribbon on which was printed:

> Save this for the Special Day
> of Richard and our daughter, Fay.
> We're planning a wedding and we're excited!
> You're the first to be invited.

If you choose, you can convey your happy message on napkins or place cards, lettered simply, Fay and Richard—Engaged!

Throughout the social world there is a custom that the father, sometime during the evening, propose a toast to his daughter and her fiancé. I can see no room for this despicable custom, or any imitation of it, in the Christian world. The holiness of marriage demands complete sobriety.

A Christian father can certainly make his joyful announcement without proposing a toast. In his own words it will probably be something like this: "I am happy to announce the engagement of my daughter, Barbara, to James Ferguson, and I know you will want to wish them good health, happiness, and God's blessing on their marriage."

The groom can respond simply with "Thank you very much. I am the luckiest and happiest man alive!"

Then the guests will want to extend a congratulatory handclasp with a "God bless you!" or, "I know you will be very happy"; or, "I'm so happy for you both!" The word "congratulations" is never used when speaking to the bride-elect.

Now What Happens?

Socially it is up to your future in-laws to respond with some kind of a "we're-glad-about-this" gesture. This gesture may be an invitation to dinner extended to the bride and her family. It may be a handwritten note from the prospective mother-in-law. It may be a telephone call from the groom's family, offering to help with the wedding plans, and especially offering to give the rehearsal dinner.

This gesture is usually made within a day or two following the official announcement of the engagement.

If no gesture is made within a week or so, don't pout about it. Maybe your future in-laws simply don't know what is expected of them. Maybe they think they are already well acquainted with you and your family and, therefore, no official "meeting" is necessary. Maybe—all kinds of things.

Give them the benefit of the doubt. Go into a tactful huddle with the groom and decide how to get the two families into a happy working relationship. I admit frankly to you that I can find no modern etiquette that decrees this, but I have read in a wonderful old book on human relations that a man named Jesus once said, "Whosoever shall compel thee to go a mile, go with him twain" (Matt. 5:41).

3

Decisions! Decisions!

It's time now to give specific answers to the questions which have been buzzing around in your brain for weeks:

Where shall the wedding be?

What kind of wedding should I have?

Who will pay for it?

What shall I wear?

What shall he wear?

You will naturally decide these things for yourself—with the aid of your parents, your pastor, and a *little* aid from the groom. Most bridegrooms have at first a strange phobia of church weddings with all their pomp and trimmings. They are especially "afraid" of all those people. The same youthful extrovert who will play a guitar and sing wildly at a hootenanny in front of hundreds can give you at least twelve good reasons why he cannot be married in public, why his knees will turn to butter, why he will shake like an aspen leaf, and why his voice will completely leave him. My advice to you is: Don't pay any attention to him.[1] Unless he screams and kicks and otherwise makes it positively plain that he will not participate in a big church wedding, proceed with *your* plans—

---

[1] My dear Husband, forgive me for this subversive antimale advice, but I remember well how YOU protested—and then how you stood calmly at the altar smiling at me as MY buttery knees brought me toward you.

full speed ahead! The irony of it all is, when you actually come to that glad hour, you are likely to be more nervous than he! And for all his protestations, he will wait placidly at the altar, actually enjoying the limelight. So, listen to his twelve good reasons—then shrug them off—and on with the plans!

Where Shall the Wedding Be?

The church.—"How lovely are thy dwellings, O Lord of hosts." The plans you are now making will soon become realities. And the realities will soon become memories. There is no memory more beautiful in the mind of woman than that of her own wedding—and the more sacred, the more worshipful it is, the more beautiful the memory. So, if at all possible, be married in your own church. If your own church is too small to accommodate the guests you will invite, then "borrow" a church. You can make arrangements to use a larger church of your denomination conveniently located.[2]

You do not have to spend a lot of money to have a church wedding. For the informal church wedding you may wear a simple street-length dress or suit and hat, and carry a bouquet. The men may wear business suits. And you do not have to have a reception. You, your families, and your wedding party may receive guests in the foyer after the wedding. Don't give up having a church wedding just because of the expense involved until you have talked it over with your pastor.

The home.—Perhaps in your mind you have a storybook picture of a lovely bride descending a spiral staircase into her living room. A string quartet renders the wedding march from a corner near the fireplace. But most of us do not have spiral staircases, and if you are going to go to the trouble to engage a string quartet, you may as well have the full church wedding. Nevertheless, a home wedding can be beautiful and worshipful. If you are married at home, don't have your father break his back by carry-

---

[2] But don't choose a church just because you want a more weddingish church. And if it is necessary to use another sanctuary, check first into all policies and financial requirements.

ing all of the living room furniture out to the garage. Leave it be! A "furnitureless" room has a peculiar unlived-in look about it. It is unnatural to say the least.

The parsonage.—If it is a simple, no-fuss wedding you wish, you can gather up your families and wedding party and hie yourselves over to the parsonage (rectory, manse, or vicarage). This has distinct advantages in that the minister's wife will have to dust and vacuum her living room and your living room can keep its cluttered, corsage-box look that belongs in a house when a daughter is being married.

If your minister's wife is like I am, she will not object to giving the magazines on the coffee table a little extra flourish. She loves a wedding in her home. Who else is privileged in the middle of an ironing or mirror-polishing to stop and enjoy a wedding right in her own living room? I like weddings so much that I always try to keep the living room spotless in anticipation of one. You may not be able to walk through my family room or kitchen, but you can get married in my living room any old time of day, and I'd be glad to have you. If I know you are coming—and I usually do—I will even bake a cake, bring down the miniature bride and groom from the top shelf in the cabinet, get out the best linen napkins, and stir up a bowl of punch. I enjoy doing these things. Most ministers' wives do.

Garden, patio, cave, or any other natural setting.—If you love the romance and fragrance of your father's rose garden and if you're a real gambler at heart, you can plan an outdoor wedding. But if you do plan to be married in the rose garden, have the living room set—just in case of rain.

Some of the most colorful underground formations ever seen anywhere are near where we live, in the hills of Missouri. This Lake of the Ozarks tourist attraction is called Bridal Cave. It is as lovely a cave as you will find. One of the rooms resembles a cathedral. There is a distinct arching of the ceiling, a natural pulpit, and a beautiful onyx stalactite-stalagmite pipe organ forming a backdrop for it all. In this room nearly four hundred weddings have been performed, beginning centuries ago with the wedding of Princess Irona of the Little Hills tribe of Osage Indians.

Why on earth would anyone want to be married in a cave? I used to ask myself. But recently I had occasion to ask a pretty bride who was being married in the cave—by my husband, incidentally. They wanted to be married quietly, she said, away from home, but not in a strange minister's home. They wanted some place to which they could return sentimentally on their anniversaries—a place where, unnoticed by other people, they could relive the beauty of their wedding.

I watched the ceremony. My husband, who had been talked into this adventure by a deacon's son—the number one guide in the cave—outdid himself. The service was simple, beautiful, and *sacred*. I came away with the conviction that a wedding could be holy almost anywhere.

But I could not help wanting to tell all the couples who have been married in our living room that they are most welcome to come back on their anniversaries, or any other time, and enjoy the memories of their parsonage weddings. Some have already done this. A couple who had been married by our Christmas tree years before saw a new season's yule lights in our window and came in out of the snow to linger again. We discreetly disappeared into the kitchen to make them a cup of coffee. Leaving them with their memories, we were glad that their marriage was so full and rich and happy that they liked to think about its beginning.

Of course, you never know when the church is likely to sell the dear old familiar house and build a new air-conditioned, three-bedroom brick with family room and den. But it's really not a big risk to take. And, if it should happen, the minister would, no doubt, be happy to recite the ceremony again by his new fireplace, thus creating brand-new memories for you.

What Kind of Wedding Yours?

Weddings, like good filet mignons, come in three degrees of "doneness."

There's the *rare* or informal wedding, the *medium* or semiformal wedding, and the *well-done* or formal wedding.

What you and your bridal party wear, more than any other factor, determines the degree of formality of your wedding. I've compiled a list for you, but remember that even these rigid rules are flexible according to locale and even from church to church in the same locale. So study my list carefully, and then shut the book! Don't go by it until you have checked its accuracy with the bridal shop where you purchase your wedding gown and the rental shop which provides the menswear. And, check with your pastor or his secretary about your church's customs.

For my list, I'll start with the simplest.

Informal

Any time of day or evening the bride may choose to wear a dressy, street-length dress or suit and a dressy hat. Her one attendant would dress accordingly. The men wear business suits, or in summer, white suits, if they have them. Flowers may be small nosegay bouquets or corsages, depending on your taste, and simple, white boutonnieres. You may have a basket or two of flowers in the altar and candles if you wish.

Semiformal Daytime

I don't care very much for the prefix "semi." I tend to see things in distinct shades of *either* and *or*. How a hospital room can be, for instance, *semi*private is beyond my comprehension. It is either private or it is not. But it's perfectly acceptable in the social world to talk about semiformal weddings, so let's talk about them.[8]

The bride.—Long white gown in any number of beautiful styles. No train. Other books say "no veil." This book says, if you want a veil have one. The veil is a symbol of submission and modesty, and once the groom learns that, he will insist on a veil, proper or not. It is proper to wear a short veil, even with a street-length

---

[8] In wedding lingo, semiformal actually means that the bride can be as formal as she pleases without the wedding party's following suit.

wedding dress. And in my system of logic, it doesn't make a great deal of difference whether the sun or the moon shines on it.

The experts also say that you don't have to wear white. If your complexion goes ghostly with the donning of white, how about pastel pink or blue? But I insist—wear *white*. Adjust your complexion, not the color of your wedding gown. If you do wear pink or blue or jade green, the old maid guests are going to spend at least three afternoons a week for the next three weeks discussing *why* you didn't wear white, and, according to their logic, it won't have a thing to do with your complexion!

Of course, if it is a second wedding, no white is preferable—and no veil!

The maid or matron of honor and bridesmaids.—Colorful dresses the same length or shorter than the bride's. Headdress of bows, bonnets, or blossoms and in their hands a fan or a flower. In selecting a pattern for your bridesmaids' dresses it is well to choose one that gives attention to the dress back. It is the back view the guests will have while the wedding party is at the altar. So, keep this in mind and choose bustles, bows, or trainish overskirts.

Mothers of the bride and groom.—Dressy, street-length dresses or suits and hats of solid fabric in preference to print. The groom will provide corsages for these honored women.

Women guests.—Same as the mothers of the bride and groom, except no flowers.

The men in the wedding party.—Dark suits, preferably all the same color. White suits may be worn in summer, or dark jackets with white trousers.

Semiformal Evening

The bride.—Same as semiformal daytime. With veil.

Maid or matron of honor and bridesmaids.—Same as semiformal daytime.

Mothers.—Same, except if they wish they may wear floor-length dresses. They both must wish it, however, and the mother of the bride's wishes have priority.

Women guests.—Street-length dresses, appropriate accessories.
The men.—Dinner jackets, black ties, boutonnieres.
Men guests.—Business suits.

Formal Daytime (before 6:00 P.M.)

The bride.—Long, white traditional wedding gown with or without a train. See notes about color under semiformal and choose a white gown.

A matching veil is attached to a hat, tiara, crown, or wreath.

Gloves are necessary only if gown has short sleeves. There are special wedding mitts available at bridal shops and department stores, which lend themselves to the ring-giving portion of the wedding ceremony.

Shoes should be satin slippers. Be certain they are comfortable.

Carry flowers according to your taste. It may be a small arrangement atop a Bible. It may be a larger bouquet. It may be a single long-stemmed rose. It may *not* be a corsage. (See chapter 8 about decorations.)

A string of pearls or pendant. Sometimes the bride's jewelry is a gift of the groom. No earrings, please. Don't even wear your watch. There should be nothing whatever to detract from your wedding costume. Your engagement ring is worn on your right hand during the wedding ceremony.

Maid or matron of honor and bridesmaids.—Pretty dresses, long or short, usually the same color or shades of the same color. The maid of honor's dress is somewhat fancier or a different color, or she carries a larger or different color bouquet (see chapter 8).

Short veils, picture hats, or wreaths in keeping with the style and material of their dresses and the season, are appropriate.

If dresses have short sleeves, gloves may be white or the same color as the dresses, and shoes should be dyed to match preferably.

All should wear the same jewelry except for engagement rings and wedding rings, which are always worn by engaged or married members of the wedding party. Sometimes the bride presents each bridesmaid with a single strand of pearls or a pendant. These should be worn at the wedding, if the bride has so planned.

Mothers of the bride and groom.—Long or street-length dresses which will harmonize with each other and with the general color scheme of the wedding. No black, white, or drab gray. Dressy hats and gloves should match the costume. (White gloves may be worn.) The groom will send appropriate corsages.

Shoes, bag, and jewelry must complement the costumes.

Women guests wear very dressy, street-length dresses, hats, gloves, and appropriate accessories. No corsages unless the women belong to the wedding party. And nothing that will detract from the bride's dress—like a swirl of white organza worn over three taffeta petticoats.

The groom.—Cutaway jacket, striped trousers, and light waistcoat or, Oxford jacket and striped trousers. Accessories include black shoes and socks, stiff white shirt and wing collar; gray silk ascot or four-in-hand tie; a silk hat if you go to that kind of church; white gloves to the church but not during the ceremony; and a small white flower, traditionally from the bridal bouquet. It depends though on what is in the bridal bouquet. A man can look perfectly virile with a carnation in his buttonhole, but I get a kind of uneasy feeling when I see a man wearing a gardenia. I don't care if it did come from the bride's bouquet!

The groom's shoes must be new and black—black tops and black bottoms. I once sat by a man on a plane who was returning home from his son's wedding in the East. His whole life was ruined— well, that day anyway—because of his son's shoe soles. He had brought his son up to be ultraproper. Had even taught him to wrap his own cummerbund—none of this hook and eye business for that elegant young man. But on the day of his wedding some prankster had painted the soles of the groom's shoes bright red. The father of the groom sat proudly through most of the ceremony, beaming with pride in this wonderful specimen of propriety that he had prepared for this hour—until his son approached the kneeling bench, revealing his bright red soles, and a wave of stifled laughter rippled through the congregation. So, new shoes—no holes in soles—and no red soles, please!

The ushers or groomsmen.—Follow the groom's example in dress. The ushers usually keep their white (or gray) gloves on while performing their duties and while participating in the wedding. The groom and best man remove their gloves for the ceremony.

Formal Evening

The bride, maid-of-honor, bridesmaids, and the bride and groom's mothers' attire is the same as for the formal daytime wedding.

Women guests should wear long or short dinner dresses with appropriate accessories and hats.

The groom, best man, ushers, and fathers of the bride and groom wear white tie and tails or the white dinner jacket and black trousers are acceptable, especially in the South or anywhere there is likely to be a hot summer evening.

Men guests should dress like the groom (no boutonnieres) or wear dinner jackets with black ties.

Additional Tips on Dress

The bride.—Have a soft nonshowy hair style. If you have to have a new permanent, get this a month or so before the wedding. Have a shampoo and set on your wedding day. Be sure your hairdresser styles your hair so your headdress will fit beautifully and comfortably.

Choose undergarments that are both pretty and comfortable. Crinolines are more graceful than hoops and easier to manage. If they tend to scratch, wear a short soft half-slip underneath. Practice walking in them around home, particularly upstairs and down again. It is better not to sit on the crinolines unless it is absolutely necessary.

Nurses wear white stockings. Brides don't. Wear pale sheer stockings.

It is the bride's responsibility to provide the ring bearer's pillow and the flower girl's decorative basket. Fortunate is the bride who has a grandmother or aunt who will make these items. The same grandmother or aunt, already supplied with satin and lace, may also make a cover for your own black Bible if you prefer to carry it rather than a new white one. And to save the expense of a special wedding knife, she can cover the handle of an ordinary cake knife with satin ribbon, affixing a few streamers and a lace rosette or two. Actually, no one will notice whether you use a sterling silver slicer or a masquerading butcher knife. Who looks at the handle of the knife when the bride and groom are cutting the cake?

You may want to be traditional, complete with the "something old, something new" bit. The something new is easy, and the something old may be grandmother's veil, or your own string of pearls. The something borrowed may be gloves or a handkerchief. The touch of blue could be the lace on your petticoat or a sapphire pendant, but it is usually a fancy, blue garter, The "sixpence in your shoe" can be anything from an Indianhead penny to a shiny new dime. Don't let anyone tell you it must be a sixpence. In the first place, it's your wedding and your shoe and your penny. In the second place, where would you get a sixpence, unless your fiancé happens to be in the United States Navy and is thoughtful enough to pick one up for you in Scotland.

The one thing which you should not let influence your choice of formal, semiformal, or informal wedding is the type of reception. A Christian bride can have a lovely formal wedding with proper dress in proper setting, and when it's over, it's over. It is ludicrous to assume that one cannot have a formal wedding without an orchestra for dancing and champagne for drinking at the reception. A wedding is a wedding and a reception is a reception. While a wedding should influence the type of reception you will have, a reception should not influence the type of wedding you will have. That's something like allowing the palomino to be pulled by the circus wagon.

Weddingitis

There is a too-common malady among brides-to-be which might be called weddingitis. Its symptoms include exhaustion, nervousness, insomnia, and irritability. It is caused by a virus which has just recently been isolated—wedding pressure. Some brides have been catapulted almost into shock by it, but you won't be. You'll be prepared.

You will discover that as soon as your engagement announcement appears, people who never had anything to say to you before suddenly say the strangest things:

"But my dear, THEY just aren't making wedding gowns these days under five hundred dollars!"

"NOBODY serves *petit fours* at a wedding reception!"

"You surely don't plan a reception without hiring an orchestra. EVERYONE has an orchestra."

"NOBODY has ever decorated that huge church with fewer than twelve baskets of very large flowers!"

Don't be shocked or embarrassed by these remarks. Recognize them for exactly what they are—the gross exaggerations of high-pressure salesmanship. You are not *everyone* and you can be *nobody* if you wish. And *they* aren't planning *your* wedding. Never forget for a single minute that you are the customer. You can end these nonsensical conversations post haste by smiling sweetly and exclaiming, "Really? How interesting! That just isn't what I had in mind." Then, without further ado, turn and walk quickly to another shop—where the salespeople are really interested in *your* wedding.

An occasional bride-to-be is even thrown into a case of weddingitis by the mail she receives. Every day the postman comes burdened with a new supply of brochures and sales letters, urging you to buy everything from wedding pictures to wedding cake. If the item is one you are shopping for, examine the brochure or read the letter. If it isn't, simply file it immediately—in that large, round wicker file that sits under your desk.

And don't let yourself be a "Winnie-the-Pooh" bride—always singing a complaining song. Complaints from brides about wedding pressures and wedding preliminaries always strike me as being a little ridiculous. Consider these bridal utterances:

"I'm simply exhausted from showers. All those packages to open!" *Oh, what a pity!*

"We were absolutely forced to spend an extra thousand dollars on the wedding!" *Really? Who held the gun?*

"We simply couldn't arrange the rehearsal dinner for less than twenty-five dollars per person!" *Oh? Where did you try?*

This is your wedding. Your attitude toward your plans and your state-of-mind in carrying through with those plans should be guided by inner calm, not outer confusion. If you remember this, it can make the difference between nightmares and pleasant dreams throughout the busy days and nights to come.

The Wedding Budget

Now let's talk about money. This subject should be fun for everyone but the bride's father. As a Christian, you will certainly not want to be extravagant in the planning of your wedding. But you will not want to be miserly either. We've reached a peculiar plateau of put-on-the-dogness in our society in which many people actually expect a daughter's wedding to equal a year's salary. This is, indeed, a sorry state of affairs. I hope that you won't take advantage of your father's love for you by begging him to spend beyond his means. On the other hand, your wedding is a once-in-a-lifetime experience and your parents will want to put into it as much as they reasonably can, depending usually on how many sisters you have and on other circumstances. The bride's father foots the bill for nearly all of the wedding expenses, namely:

The announcement party.

Invitations, announcements, other stationery items, and postage.

The bride's wedding gown and trousseau.

Church decorations and most of the flowers (see chapter 10).

Fees (if required) for organist, sexton, soloist.

Photographs and recordings of the occasion.

Insurance while the wedding gifts are on display.

Hotel accommodations, if needed, for any of the bride's attendants from out of town.

The bridesmaids' luncheon, unless a friend assumes this responsibility.

The trousseau tea.

The rehearsal party or dinner *unless* the groom's family offers to give it—and they usually do.

In addition, the bride (and here goes another hand reaching down into dear old Dad's pocket) pays for:

The groom's gift.

The groom's ring.

Gifts for the bridal attendants.

Her medical checkup and premarital tests.

The guest book and the wedding memoir and gift books.

The groom pays for:

The engagement ring.

The bride's wedding ring and flowers and flowers for both mothers.

The marriage license.

His medical tests or examinations.

The bride's gift (usually jewelry).

Gifts for the best man, ushers, and ringbearer; gloves and ties worn by the men in the wedding party.

Hotel accommodations, if needed, for men in the wedding party from out of town; and the fee to the minister. Actually, the phrase "monetary gift" is more pertinent than "fee." This gift is usually ten dollars or more, depending on the location and the size of the wedding and whether or not the couple belong to the minister's church. Don't ask the minister what his fee is. He doesn't have a set fee and can't tell you. His wife won't tell you either. If you really want to know what he usually gets, ask his secretary. She will tell you.

The groom also provides the future home and all the major furniture and equipment.

When it comes right down to admitting it, it costs a lot to get married—even with help. The *help* is that:

The bride's attendants usually pay for their own dresses, shoes, and hats—everything but flowers.

All of the members of the wedding party present gifts to the couple—and this is a fact not to be sneezed at!

If members of the wedding party come from afar, they must pay their own transportation expenses.

Often, too, friends give luncheons, dinners, and showers.

And the groom's parents, who through the years have been joking at wedding receptions about how perfectly lovely to have five sons and no daughters, suddenly stop smiling and realize that they are responsible for:

Their own wedding clothes and additional clothes for the groom's mother for prewedding festivities.

Their own travel expenses and hotel bills.

The rehearsal dinner (not compulsory but it surely is manna in the wilderness for the bride's family).

And, of course, the nicest wedding present that whatever money is left over can buy.

The important thing to remember about finance is this: Sit down with your dad at the very beginning and establish a budget. Then make every effort to stay within it, even if it means no reception and two less bridesmaids. Be honest with yourself and with your father, and you will probably steer clear of pitfalls and stay out of trouble—well, out of *bankruptcy* anyway.

4

Seek Your Minister's Advice

By far the most important member of your wedding party is the minister. Marriage is a religious rite. Your government recognizes this when it gives ministers the authority to marry persons it has licensed. In addition to the legal responsibility placed on the minister, he has spiritual responsibilities relevant to the nature of your marriage. It is his utmost desire that you contract a lasting, happy marriage. For this reason, he will either want to counsel with you in every detail concerning your coming marriage, or he will refer you to a professional marriage counselor. The counselor and the minister both want to be sure that you realize fully *all* of the responsibilities of marriage.

In order that you may meditate on some of these things beforehand, here is a list of subjects your minister will probably want to discuss with you in your premarital counseling sessions. I have included some Scripture passages concerning marriage for your mind and soul to digest.

Man did not invent marriage as a means of satisfying his physical, spiritual, and emotional desires. God did. Marriage is God's plan to further man's happiness, for he said, "It is not good that the man should be alone; I will make him a helper fit for him" (Gen. 2:18, RSV).

So he made woman and instituted the marriage relationship.

24

Because God did this, this relationship should be regarded as holy and should be deemed eternal.

Responsibilities of the husband.—God did not just create woman and stop. He made some plans for her and established rules by which her husband should be guided in his relationships with her. "Therefore a man leaves his father and his mother and cleaves to his wife, and they become one flesh" (Gen. 2:24, RSV).

And God said, through Moses:

Thou shalt have no other gods before me. Thou shalt not make unto thee any graven image. . . . Thou shalt not take the name of the Lord thy God in vain. . . . Remember the sabbath day, to keep it holy. . . . Honour thy father and thy mother. . . . Thou shalt not kill. Thou shalt not commit adultery. Thou shalt not steal. Thou shalt not bear false witness against thy neighbor. . . . Thou shalt not covet (Ex. 20:3–16).

The Lord our God is one Lord: And thou shalt love the Lord thy God with all thine heart, and with all thy soul, and with all thy might. And these words, which I command thee this day, shall be in thine heart: And thou shalt teach them diligently unto thy children, and shalt talk of them when thou sittest in thine house, and when thou walkest by the way, and when thou liest down, and when thou risest up (Deut. 6:4–7).

The apostle Paul wrote: "Husbands, love your wives, even as Christ also loved the church, and gave himself for it" (Eph. 5:25).

Responsibilities of the wife.—About a good wife, the Bible says:

A good wife who can find?
    She is far more precious than jewels.
The heart of her husband trusts in her,
    and he will have no lack of gain.
She does him good, and not harm,
    all the days of her life.
She seeks wool and flax,
    and works with willing hands.
She is like the ships of the merchant,
    she brings her food from afar.

She rises while it is yet night
    and provides food for her household
    and tasks for her maidens.
She considers a field and buys it;
    with the fruit of her hands she plants a vineyard.
She girds her loins with strength
    and makes her arms strong.
She perceives that her merchandise is profitable.
    Her lamp does not go out at night.
She puts her hands to the distaff,
    and her hands hold the spindle.
She opens her hand to the poor,
    and reaches out her hands to the needy.
She is not afraid of snow for her household,
    for all her household are clothed in scarlet.
She makes herself coverings;
    her clothing is fine linen and purple.
Her husband is known in the gates,
    when he sits among the elders of the land.
She makes linen garments and sells them;
    she delivers girdles to the merchant.
Strength and dignity are her clothing,
    and she laughs at the time to come.
She opens her mouth with wisdom,
    and the teaching of kindness is on her tongue.
She looks well to the ways of her household,
    and does not eat the bread of idleness.
Her children rise up and call her blessed;
    her husband also, and he praises her:
"Many women have done excellently,
    but you surpass them all."
Charm is deceitful, and beauty is vain,
    But a woman who fears the Lord is to be praised (Prov.
        31:10–30, RSV).

The apostle Paul wrote: "Wives, be subject to your husbands as to the Lord. For the husband is the head of the wife as Christ is the head of the church, his body, and is himself its Savior. As the church is subject to Christ, so let wives also be subject in everything to their husbands" (Eph. 5:22–24, RSV).

Again the apostle Paul wrote: "Put on then, as [the garments that suit] God's chosen ones, holy and beloved, compassion, kindness, lowliness, meekness, and patience, forbearing one another and, if one has a complaint against another, forgiving each other; as the Lord has forgiven you, so you also must forgive. And above all these put on love, which binds everything together in perfect harmony" (Col. 3:12–14, RSV).

Joint responsibilities.—It is very important that your two hearts beat as one in the matter of religious faith, that you serve the Lord together, that you work together in the *same* church, that you establish a family altar, and that you bring your children up "in the nurture and admonition of the Lord" (Eph. 6:4).

Your pastor will discuss this subject at length with you.

Some questions about finance you will want to ask yourselves before talking with your pastor are:

Are we willing to live within the income we will have?

Will it be necessary for the wife to work?

Am I really willing, if necessary, to accept a lower standard of living than I've been accustomed to in my parents' home?

Am I truly unselfish?

What portion of our income will we want to give to God through our church?

To aid your discussions about the place of sex in the marriage relationship, your minister may want to use either one of the following, or similar guides: *Premarital Counseling Guide for Pastors,* prepared by Granger E. Westberg, Chaplain, Augustana Hospital, Chicago, Illinois; *Marriage Counselor's Manual and Sex Knowledge Inventory,* developed by Gelolo McHugh, Family Life Publications, Durham, North Carolina.

What should your attitude be toward your future in-laws? What will you call them? Will they interfere with your marriage? If so, what will your reaction be?

I would like to add a personal aside here about in-laws. The easiest way in the world to get along with them is simply to love them. Learning to love my husband's mom and dad posed no problem for me, for I already loved them. The man who is my

father-in-law now was my pastor for most of my growing-up life.
I can't even remember when I began to love him or Mom. And as
for brother and sister type in-laws, as an only child I resolved
early to marry into a large family. Every Christmas and Fourth of
July, which are reunion times for the Swadleys, I realize fully what
a terribly good job I did of fulfilling my childhood desire! What a
big, happy, noisy family I married! And I love them as I would my
own brothers and sisters. They ARE my own—nieces, nephews,
cousins, aunts, and uncles. We have never had any "getting along"
type problems, and even if we should I am sustained by the knowledge that "love is patient and kind; love is not jealous or boastful;
it is not arrogant or rude. Love does not insist on its own way; it is
not irritable or resentful; it does not rejoice at wrong, but rejoices
in the right. Love bears all things, believes all things, hopes all
things, endures all things" (1 Cor. 13:4–7, RSV).

This is the best advice the world has ever heard for getting along
with people, and in-laws ARE people—very *special* people.

Ethics Concerning the Selection of a Minister

There are some ethics to follow concerning the selection of the
minister who will perform your wedding ceremony. It strikes me as
one of the gross inconsistencies of our day that many people who
will strain every etiquette nerve to be socially proper will shrug off
the matter of ministerial ethics with never so much as a passing
thought.

The pastor of the bride is usually asked to officiate. This is not,
however, an ironclad rule.

If the bride has a close relative who is a minister, she should
certainly choose him. Ministerial ethics decree that she inform her
pastor of her desire, and he will then invite the relative to officiate at
her wedding in his church.

If the groom's father is a minister, and the bride has no close
relative who is, she should certainly choose her future father-in-
law.

This rule applies to other close relatives, too. A fond uncle of either the bride or groom might be chosen, but in any case, the pastor should be immediately informed of the bride's desire and should have a part in the invitation to the guest minister.

If a minister who is a relative and lives some distance away has been chosen, he will often ask the pastor to handle the counseling part of the premarital planning. Sometimes, even when he is near, he will do this, because a prospective bride and groom will probably talk more freely with a pastor than with a minister relative.

In fact the bride might specify this in her first session with her pastor. "I have a close uncle who is a minister and I would like for him to perform the actual ceremony. Would you invite him for me please? But, I'd like you to handle the counseling. We could talk more freely with you." Your pastor should respond nicely to this sort of invitation. He is ethically bound to. But if he doesn't, you'll be extra glad you've got old Uncle Minister!

A former pastor should almost never be asked. You would create problems for him as well as yourself, for he is under the ministerial system of ethics to sever all old ties—no matter how dear—and move bag, baggage, heart, and soul to the new church field without so much as a backward glance.

In a church that has an associate pastor or a youth pastor, you will probably be creating difficulties for yourself if you invite one of them to officiate rather than your pastor. Some pastors don't care. They want you to place faith and trust in their assistants, just as you place faith and trust in them. And should that faith and trust develop into *preference,* that's fine. The pastor is a busy man anyway.

So, walk softly. Every church is different, and I discovered from a questionnaire which was returned to me from ministers in over forty states that almost every pastor is different.

You can usually "feel" your pastor's desires and act accordingly. If you can't, ask the minister's secretary. If she likes to keep the church wheels running with all ball bearings in place, she will discreetly advise you.

When my husband is not chosen to perform the ceremony, he

prefers to do the counseling, and then enjoy the wedding service as any other guest. He can, as a baritone, render a near professional "Lord's Prayer" and has done so for special people, but he really enjoys the opportunity to be just a wedding guest for a change.

Church Policies for Weddings

Many churches have policy statements, forms to fill out, instructions to florists, musicians and caterers. Whether your pastor performs your ceremony or not, it is his responsibility to see that your wedding is planned within the framework of the church policy. Here is a sample application and policy statement.

Dear Bride-elect: We are happy that you contemplate being married in the church. We shall do our best to make this holy and happy occasion all that you wish it to be. Below is the form of the application to be followed by those contemplating the use of any room for weddings. The form is one somewhat based on those used in various churches, and has been approved by the Executive Committee of the church. The purpose is to assist you and to provide staff members with information necessary for orderliness.

Wedding Application
(subject to conditions on the attached sheet)

Wedding Date: _____ Hour _____

Rehearsal Date: _____ Hour _____

Minister: _____ Phone No. _____

(If minister other than or in addition to the pastor or assistant pastor is desired, the pastor should be requested to invite the minister desired.)

Organist: _____ Vocalist: _____

(If other than church organist, give telephone number.)

Florist and Phone No.: _____

Caterer and Phone No.: _____

Groom Elect: _____ Phone No.: _____

Present Address: _____

Address after Marriage: _____

Church Affiliation: _____ Where: _____

Parents: _____ Address: _____

Church Affiliation: _____ Where: _____

Bride Elect: _____ Phone No.: _____

Address: _____

Church Affiliation: _____ Where: _____

Parents: _____ Address: _____

Church Affiliation: _____ Where: _____

Church Facilities Desired: _____

I have read the conditions provided on the attached sheet of this application and agree to abide by same if I am permitted the use of these facilities and to make every effort to insure that my guests will do likewise.

_____
                                                    Applicant's Signature

Bring or mail to: _____

Approved: _____

Date: _____

CONDITIONS
Please Read Carefully

Schedule of charges for weddings to partially cover the expense to the church of providing facilities desired:

1. If either the bride or groom is a member of the _____ Church or the child of a member:
   a. Sanctuary (janitor service, including use of steps) $10.00
   b. Chapel (janitor service if steps are used) 10.00
      (janitor service without the use of steps) 5.00
   c. Church parlor .... Optional
      (janitor service required) 5.00
   d. Janitor service if wedding is on Saturday 10.00
2. If neither the bride nor groom is a member of the _____ Church or the child of a member:
   a. Sanctuary
      (1) Air conditioning (cooling, heating, circulating) $25.00
      (2) Janitor service with use of steps 20.00
      (3) Janitor service without the use of steps 10.00
      (4) Janitor service if on Saturday 20.00
   b. Chapel
      (1) Air conditioning (cooling, heating, circulating) $15.00
      (2) Janitor service if steps are used 20.00
      (3) Janitor service without the steps 10.00
      (4) Janitor service if on Saturday 20.00
   c. Parlor 3.00
      (janitor service) 5.00

3. If church facilities are used for wedding receptions, the following conditions must be observed:
   a. No receptions are held on Saturdays and Sundays.
   b. No food or drinks are to be served in the church parlor. Smoking is also forbidden in the parlor. The parlor is to be used for the receiving line only.
   c. No intoxicants of any kind are to be served in connection with reception.
   d. The church hostess must supervise the use of facilities; even though a caterer may actually direct and "serve." Whether the church hostess directs and "serves" is upon invitation of the bride and optional with the hostess. The church does not serve wedding receptions. It makes facilities available under supervision of the hostess.
   e. Fees:
      (1) Church hostess $10.00 honorarium for each reception.
      (2) $5.00 for each maid or janitor used in connection with reception. (One janitor is required if in . . . lobby; two janitors are required if in dining room.)
   f. The furniture in the parlor is not to be moved.
4. Neither rice, confetti, nor other material may be thrown inside any of the church buildings.
5. Intoxicants are not permitted in any of the church buildings. To avoid embarrassment, it is suggested that these rules be called to the attention of all members of the wedding party.
6. In scheduling a wedding the church staff will make every effort to avoid conflicts; however, if such should occur, use of the facilities for church-wide religious services must take preference over wedding ceremonies.
7. If other than regular church organists are used, approval must be secured from a member of the Music Committee and the pastor. (A cash gift is suggested for the organist when one of the church organists is used.)
8. Payment for facilities requested must be made at time application is presented.
9. Please provide all of the information requested on the attached sheet:

MEMORANDUM TO ALL FLORISTS

The florists of the city who have been employed in the past by wedding parties to decorate the church are usually most cooperative in every way. We delight to participate with you in a service of dignity and beauty for the bride. Occasionally, however, there have been times when the church maids and janitors have been hard pressed because of failure on the part of the florist to understand what was expected of him by the church. We take this means to advise you concerning the following resolution adopted sometime ago by the Executive Committee of the church.

BE IT RESOLVED, by the Executive Committee of _____ Church, that all florists in _____ be advised of this policy adopted by the Executive Committee in regard to decorating for weddings.

That all florists decorating for any wedding in any room of the church will be expected to leave the room in the same order in which they found it when beginning their decorating. This is to be done immediately after each wedding. The failure of any florist in the city to cooperate with this requirement will necessitate the church advising the parents involved in any prospective wedding that such florist is not acceptable to _____ Church.

That every florist decorating for a wedding in the church shall clear with the church office the time when decorations are to be brought into the room or auditorium used for the wedding in order that there be no conflict with a meeting already scheduled.

As pastor of the church, I was requested to convey this resolution to you. I am sure that you agree that the resolution is a reasonable one. Thank you for your friendship and cooperation.

Cordially yours,

_____, Pastor

5

Who Does What

Now, having chosen the minister, let's give consideration to the other members of the wedding party—how to choose
them and what they do.

One of the bride's big problems is how to motivate bridesmaids
into functioning. Most are content to walk down the aisle, stand and
look pretty, and that's all. They do not remember that bridesmaid
means, in addition to bride's attendant, bride's "female servant." So
they do nothing whatever to assist you with your wedding preparations, rehearsal, and all that other work—unless you tell them in
detail what you want them to do.

One of the best ways I can think of is for you to tactfully show
them a copy of this book. Or better still, *give* them a copy, declaring
as you hand it over, "Just look at this clever little book I've found.
It simply tells everything about weddings." The giving of this book
will not suffice for the traditional bridesmaid's gift, but it will make
her think a little more kindly of you when she is buying eight and
one-half yards of pastel blue brocade at $3.45 per yard to make the
dress that you have asked her to wear! And it WILL get her to function as a bridesmaid, provided you weed out from all these para-
graphs what you want her to do and point it out to her with your
index finger, right hand.

Or, if you care to be more discreet, on informal white cards give

gentle instructions and insert one in each bridesmaid's book between pages ——— and ———. Thusly,

> *Caroline:*
> *Would you please — distribute
> the flowers — and see that
> Joe's Aunt Pearl has a good
> time at the reception?*
> *Thanks so much,*
> *Jane*

Now, to the specifics:

The Maid of Honor

This is the honor of honors to bestow on that person dearest to
your heart. She is usually your sister or a very close friend. If you
have been maid of honor at more than one wedding, or if you have
two very close sisters, you will just have to eenie, meenie, miney
mo them or use some sensible method of selection—and just choose
one.

The maid of honor pays for her own dress, though you select it
—also her own shoes and headdress.
She signs the marriage certificate.
She carries the groom's ring.
At the reception she stands next to the groom in the receiving
line and introduces guests to the person next to her.
She usually gives a shower for the bride.

She assists the bride in every way possible. She can be included
in the shopping excursions, arranging gifts for display, and helping

address the wedding invitations. She can serve at the trousseau tea. On the day of the wedding she will help the bride dress—if the bride desires help—either at home or church. She is the bride's tranquilizer. She will answer questions like, "Do I look all right?" with a great big enthusiastic, "You look absolutely lovely!" And, indeed, it is the responsibility of the maid of honor to keep the bride looking absolutely lovely. She is the bride's mirror, and she should make sure that every hair is in place, every fold of the veil and train is just as it should be, before they both begin that long walk down the aisle.

She never stops functioning simply to look pretty, though if she is enjoying her work, she will automatically look pretty. She functions right through the ceremony, handing over the groom's ring on cue from the minister, holding the bridal bouquet during the exchange of rings, lifting the bride's veil at the close of the ceremony, and finally straightening the bride's train for the recessional.

The matron of honor is chosen on the same basis as the maid of honor and her duties and responsibilities are the same. In a very large wedding you may have both a maid of honor and a matron of honor if you wish. If you happen to have one married sister and one single sister you can give them equal billing in your wedding.

The Bridesmaids

Bridesmaids are selected from among sisters, relatives, and close friends. If the groom has an appropriate sister, you will by all means want to invite her to be one of your bridesmaids, even if you hardly know her. You will *learn* to know her and bestowing this honor upon her might help to get your relationship off to a good "in-lawish" start.

You may have one bridesmaid, or you may have as many as eight. The more you have, the more expensive your wedding becomes, because it means one more bouquet and one more bridesmaid's gift—and, one more T-bone steak at the rehearsal dinner.

It is not absolutely necessary to have bridesmaids. I remember one lovely wedding where money was certainly no object and the bride could have had twenty bridesmaids had she wished, but she did not wish to have ANY.

She had been away from her hometown for so long that she had no close bridesmaid-type friends left. So, she brought with her her onetime college roommate who served as maid of honor and all others in the wedding party were groomsmen, mostly friends of the groom and the bride's brother. In this case, some of the groomsmen stood where the bridesmaids would ordinarily stand to give the wedding party a balanced effect. It was quite proper and pretty and tended to center all eyes on the lovely bride herself. But if it's color you wish, and *beauty,* have the bridesmaids, for loveliness of dress and loveliness of the girls themselves can add much to your wedding.

A bridesmaid pays for her own dress.

She attends all prenuptial showers, parties, and festivities.

She attends the rehearsal and follows instructions given her by the minister.

She is on hand, when required, for photographs.

Promptness is her chief virtue.

She helps entertain guests at the reception. (See chapter 14.)

If your florist simply delivers the flowers to the church, it is nice to have one bridesmaid responsible for seeing that everyone has the right bouquet and that the right corsage is pinned on the right mother ahead of time. She can also hand the boutonnieres to the head usher and ask him to see that all the male members of the wedding party are properly flowered.

Junior bridesmaids' duties are much the same as their older sisters. The only difference is that they are younger—usually between ten and fourteen. And they are usually nieces or cousins. I don't know whether queens and princesses have more nieces and cousins than anyone else, but they nearly always have a bevy of junior bridesmaids at their weddings. For you, it is not a matter of royal blood, it is a matter of taste and budget. If you have just one or two girls in this age group that you would like to use in your wedding, you might use them as candlelighters,[1] but if you, like Princess Grace and Princess Margaret, have several little kinfolk, you may want to have junior bridesmaids. The choice is yours.

The Best Man

The best man is usually the groom's father, brother, or closest friend. His duties are so multitudinous that he can easily be called the hardest working member of the wedding.

He arranges to wear what you have chosen for him. It is entirely proper for him to rent it.

He attends the rehearsal and responds to the minister's instructions.

He takes the groom's going-away clothes to the place of the reception.

He carries the luggage to the going-away car and sees that it is safely placed in the locked trunk.

He helps the groom dress for the ceremony, or more accurately, he gives him moral support while he dresses himself.

He takes care of the marriage license and the bride's wedding ring.

He delivers the minister's fee, sealed in a white envelope, which the groom has given to him in advance.

He performs whatever chauffeuring duties are necessary for bridesmaids and out-of-town guests, or he may designate this responsibility to other groomsmen.

He signs the marriage license.

Ushers

The head usher is responsible for all the other ushers. He sees that they are on time for the rehearsal and an hour early for the wedding.

---

[1] If you do use them as candlelighters, there is one very important question to consider before inviting them, and that is, "Can they reach the candles?"

He distributes the boutonnieres to the men in the wedding party, unless the florist provides a page to do this.

He follows any special instructions given him by the bride's mother about seating special people.

He coordinates the working responsibilities of all of the ushers and does everything possible to see that everything runs smoothly.

The main function of an usher is to usher. He offers his right arm to a woman guest, asking her as he does so, "Are you a friend of the bride or the groom?" [2] If she answers, "The bride," he seats her on the left side of the church. The groom's friends are seated on the right side of the church. But the ushers should use discretion and not let the church fill up lopsidedly. When either the bride or groom is a great distance from home and few friends and relatives can attend, the ushers simply seat people conveniently and efficiently, giving the church a balanced, *unnoticeable* look.

An usher does not offer his arm to a man. When a gentleman guest arrives alone, the usher walks beside him to his seat, or in some areas, in front of him.

Ushers, take note! No guest is ever seated after the bride's mother.

Ushers perform duties as designated by the minister and the head usher.

One or two may be designated to receive gifts and take them to a designated place. People aren't supposed to bring gifts to weddings, but they have a determined way of showing up in the foyer fifteen minutes before wedding time.

Two ushers may light the candles.

One will seat the groom's mother, offering her his right arm, and will return for her later.

Another will seat the bride's mother and return for her later.

Another two may close the aisle with ribbons. Ribbons, long streamers actually, are often used to seal the aisles. After the bride's

---

[2] This sounds infinitely better than the usual, "Whose side are you on?"

mother has been seated, two ushers advance to the front of the aisle
where the florist has secured the ribbons. Together they unroll the
ribbons, laying them gently on the backs of the pews and securing
them with loops on the last pew. The family and special guests who
sit in the front pews are not usually hemmed in, thus the phrase
"*behind* the ribbons." If these streamers are not used and the family
pews are marked with satin bows, then the honored phrase changes
to "*within* the ribbons."

The same two, or another two, may return to the altar to draw
out the white canvas aisle cloth.

The ushers may usher out the honored guests, the grandmothers,
aunts, housemothers and special people, and the head usher should
designate in advance who gets whom when.

And they may usher out all of the wedding guests, releasing them
a row at a time from front of church to back. I like this orderly system, especially if the reception is in the same building.

You will need one usher for every thirty or forty guests or one to
balance every bridesmaid in the wedding party. If you have fewer
ushers than responsibilities, you simply combine responsibilities.
And if you have fewer responsibilities than ushers, or have too
many ushers to balance the bridesmaids, just leave a few ushers out
of the processional and have them seated on a designated back pew.

If formal wedding pictures are to be made, the ushers make themselves available. Otherwise, and much to be preferred, they mingle
among the people at the reception and help to entertain the guests!
A huddle of ushers at a reception is an unnecessary and unfortunate
situation. The ushers have had time to huddle at the rehearsal
dinner, before the wedding, and now is the time to unhuddle and
mingle.

The Candlelighters

The candlelighters, if other than ushers, are usually young girls.
They pay for their own dresses, which usually are modified versions
of the bridesmaids' dresses. They often wear wrist corsages. To

organ accompaniment, they light the long white tapers, either with special candlelighters or an extra candle.

You may prefer to have the candles already burning when guests arrive and not have anyone light them as a part of the service. This is certainly permissible and cheaper, for it saves a corsage or two, a gift or two, and a place or two at the rehearsal dinner.

The Flower Girl

The flower girl is the most precious little girl you know and love and want to include in your wedding. She may or may not be related to you or the groom.

Minimum age doesn't matter a great deal, but maturity certainly does. If you want to include children in your wedding, choose children who will perform their responsibilities as capably as little adults.

The flower girl carries a small basket of petals, which she drops in the path of the bride. She walks immediately in front of the bride in the processional and immediately behind the bride and groom in the recessional. And if you are blessed with twin nieces or two pretty little neighbors, you may have two flower girls.

Decide whether you want the flower girl, ring bearer, or pages to actually stand at the altar. They may simply be seated with their parents in a front pew after performing their duties.

You may want to include them in the rehearsal dinner. Most books say not, but I think if a child is mature enough to perform as a flower girl before a church full of people, she is mature enough to be invited to dinner. Of course, you must also invite her parents. Her parents are responsible for her dress, and her mother is usually her representative at your prenuptial parties. The bride usually provides the petal basket, and then keeps it for a bun basket, a flower basket, or an Easter basket for her firstborn.

The Ring Bearer

The ring bearer carries a ring on a satin and lace pillow. For obvious reasons, it is usually not *the* ring. And even when the bride is brave enough to let him carry the real ring, she sees that it is securely pinned to his pillow. The ring bearer walks directly in front of the flower girl in the processional and usually with her on the way out. You may or may not include him in the rehearsal dinner. Only last summer I sat across from a mature five-year-old boy whose elegant table manners put some of the ushers to shame. This same boy, now six, is looking forward soon to another ring-carrying responsibility; this time on condition that he doesn't have to wear short pants! He doesn't. In summer a white suit is appropriate, and in winter a dark suit. And there are many variations of the ring bearer's costume—all appropriate, according to local custom and the ring bearer's wishes.

Pages

If you have two little boys you want to use in your wedding, designate them as pages. They can help carry your train and arrange it at the altar. Actually, you don't need this help, and you're often better off without it, but it *is* picturesque. If you do use pages, it is better to have them sit down about the same time your father does. They are likely to overfunction and keep fidgeting with your train through the ceremony, unless you plan a definite time for their function to cease. The pages, flower girl, and ring bearer can function again at the reception, handing out pieces of wrapped cake or individual net bags of rice.

The Guest Book Attendant

She presides at the guest book, keeps a couple of extra pens handy, in case, and remembers to smile sweetly at the guests as they come in. She is not required to attend the rehearsal but must come at least an hour early to the wedding and take up her position in the foyer. She usually wears a street-length, dressy dress even at a formal wedding. And she can hurry people along without seeming to rush them and prevent that common wedding malady known as guest-book-bottleneck. She must not do this hurrying with words, but by the quick, efficient way she hands the pen to guests and turns the pages in the guest book. If this doesn't hurry the people along, she is allowed one or two (never more) furtive glances in the direction of the growing line, and she must remember to smile pleasantly between the furtive glances.

You may prefer to have the guest book signed during the reception.

Reception Assistants

To assist with your reception, you will want to select good, attractive friends whom you can trust to remember to take the rollers out of their hair and look their very best as they cut and serve cake, pour, or otherwise keep the party moving. The caterer, or that special aunt who has volunteered to handle your reception, will keep things moving from kitchen to serving tables, but your assistants must take it from there. And blessed are you if you do have a doting aunt who will take the reception clear out of your mother's busy hands and just plan it and DO it.

Musicians

See chapter 7 on how to select the musicians for your wedding.

The Wedding Consultant

Some bridal shops furnish wedding advice along with the display of wedding gowns, and this is good. You will need all the free advice you can get. But some establishments furnish a creature called the "wedding manager" or the "wedding consultant" or various other dubious titles. This person, for a fee, will actually plan your wedding and see that the plans are carried out step by step.

I would suggest that you not engage a wedding manager, unless you are certain that his or her taste is exactly the same as yours. If his plan conflicts with the plan of your minister you will discover yourself in the dilemma of having too many chiefs and not enough Indians. And the arguments which ensue—yellow roses versus red ones, the seating or not seating of the grandmothers, cranberry punch versus strawberry punch—will not contribute greatly to the happiness of the wedding. In this do-it-yourself era you may be far better off to read books of wedding etiquette, talk to wedding consultants, and then, with the help of your pastor, make your own plans and engage your parents, your wedding party, and anyone else you can maneuver into it, to help you carry out your plans.

I have seen a few beautiful weddings planned and executed by paid managers. But I have seen a few turned into sheer havoc. Too much emphasis on the theatrical aspects of the wedding tends invariably to detract from the more important spiritual aspect. So, do it yourself—and proceed with caution.

Family Members of the Wedding Party and What They Do

The mother of the bride.—She is the hostess at the wedding and reception.

She cooperates with the groom's mother in the planning of the rehearsal dinner.

She cooperates with the goom's mother in planning their outfits for the wedding. They should not clash, and one should not overpower the other. And both should blend with, but not imitate, the general wedding decor.

If it is the custom of your congregation to stand during the entrance of the bride, in the bride's honor, it is the bride's mother who gives this cue by standing first.

It shall also be the solemn duty of the bride's mother not to cry. Oh, she may have some sparkly eyelash length tears, but certainly not drippy, sniffly type tears. Nothing detracts so much from the beauty of a ceremony as a nose-blowing mother of the bride. She can cry herself to sleep on the wedding night should she so please, but she must squelch her public tears.

The father of the bride.—He pays the bills.

At the engagement party he announces your engagement (see chap. 2).

He gives you away.

He is host for the reception and stands in the receiving line at the reception. (He doesn't have to, but I like for him to.)

He goes to the church with you. Sometimes he does the driving and sometimes an usher does. I think it is nice for the usher to drive, so that father and daughter can spend these few moments together without having to concentrate on getting through traffic. If you are a gracious daughter, you will remember to thank him sometime during this ride for giving you this beautiful wedding. Give him a kiss as you leave the car. And it is a mark of good breeding for you to give him a parting smile when he releases you at the altar.

The mother of the groom.—She usually arranges a tea or dinner in order to introduce her prospective daughter-in-law to her friends and relatives.

She sits in the second pew, right side of church, as the wedding's most honored guest.

She stands in the receiving line at the reception.

The father of the groom.—It is not an absolute necessity, but it is nice of the groom's family to take full responsibility for the rehearsal dinner.

As a part of the receiving line, he greets all the guests at the reception.

He actually doesn't have a lot to do, but if he is a typical father of the groom, he will be mighty glad he doesn't.

Volunteers

The unavoidable, unsolicited volunteer or advice-giver is inevitable. So prepare yourself in advance.

I know a bride who was reduced to tears by the insistence of a Metropolitan opera star that he sing at her wedding. She had already planned soloists, but he assumed that anyone would rather have him. Over two or three dead bodies he sang! His style of singing was so out of place in the tiny midwestern town, it nearly ruined the wedding.

Be ready to say, "Oh, I appreciate your offer so much, but all of our plans have already been made." This does not have to be a little white lie. It can be the truth if you're on the ball and *make* all of your plans before you start discussing them with the general public.

6

Inviting Family and Friends

If the wedding is to be very small, invitations may be telephoned or handwritten informally by your mother. A handwritten invitation would follow a form like this:

DEAR JACK AND BETTY,

Elizabeth Ann and Fred Kindall are being married in the chapel of First Baptist Church on Friday, January the tenth, at three o'clock.

We hope you will both be able to come to the ceremony and afterward to the reception in our home.

Lovingly,

EDITH HILLHOUSE

If it is a larger wedding, however, you will want engraved invitations. Your stationery dealer will be most helpful in the selection of style and wording. But before you visit him, you should sit down with your mother and determine the number of guests to be invited to the wedding and the number to be invited to the reception.

It is the prerogative of the bride's family to decide how big the wedding will be and how many people will be invited to the reception. However, the bride or her mother should ask the groom's family for a list of people they would like to have invited. You may even properly designate a certain number. But, I would like to remind you that this is your first big opportunity to please your future mother-in-law, and should she present a list longer than you expected, or should she indicate that she feels the number you specified is too small, be flexible! It is far easier—and much more sensible—to persuade your dad to pay for a larger reception than to try to persuade your future mother-in-law to shorten her list. And, I cannot emphasize enough how important it is to establish a good relationship with your in-laws, even *before* the beginning.

A loose-leaf notebook is a good place to compile your multitudinous checklists, including the guest list. List the names on the left-hand side of the page, leaving ample room at the right to record acceptances, gifts, and other information you desire.

The wedding list should include:

All relatives of the bride and groom.

All close friends and neighbors of both families.

College friends.

Church friends.

Business friends of both families. (A business *friend* is different from a business *associate*. In my dozen years in the business world, I could tell the difference all by myself without having to refer to an encyclopedia.)

Members of the wedding party and their parents and wives and husbands of married members of the wedding party.

Wife of the officiating minister; and the groom's minister (if other than the bride's) and his wife.

The groom's parents are not invited by mail, but they will be flattered by your taking time out to *take* to them a wedding invitation which they will cherish as a wedding remembrance.

Also influencing the number of invitations to be ordered is the use of the "blanket" invitation—an invitation addressed to a group of people. Not too many years ago the "blanket" invitation was considered taboo by everyone. It still is by some social sororities, women's clubs, and business firms. But it is now almost universally accepted by church congregations all over the country as being the best way to invite the whole congregation without oversight. It is, of course, less expensive than sending individual invitations to all church members. Custom varies from place to place. Your minister will be your important guide here. In some churches the invitation is copied verbatim and used as a bulletin insert, while in others, the invitation is read from the pulpit as a part of the announcement portion of the worship service. In still others it is posted on a bulletin board. Sometimes a note is simply placed in the bulletin or in the church newsletter: "The congregation has received an invitation to attend the marriage of Elizabeth Young to Robert Earl Edwards on Friday, the twenty-second of May, at eight o'clock, in the sanctuary."

These details will need to be discussed and worked out before you order your invitations. If you use a blanket invitation, the number of invitations you order may be shortened by several hundred.

Once you have determined how many invitations and reception cards will be needed, visit your stationer or engraver and place your order. This should be done about two months before your wedding date.

Who Issues the Invitations?

Invitations are issued by the parents of the bride—if both parents are not living, by the one surviving, or if neither is living, by the nearest or closest relative. The generally accepted order of relationship is older brother; older sister; both grandparents, or one surviving; uncle and aunt; guardian; bride and groom issue invitations themselves; or groom's family.

Though the above is the accepted list, do not take from a guardian who has lovingly cared for you all these years the privilege of giving your wedding just because you have an older brother you may not have seen since childhood.

Be as proper as you can, but be sensibly proper.

Do You Speak "Wedding"?

There is a beautiful language belonging only to weddings and this is your once-in-a-lifetime opportunity to use it.

Honour and favour are spelled wedding-ish with the "u's" in them.

Eight-thirty disappears happily in favor of half after eight o'clock.

If the year is used (it may or may not be), it is spelled out.

If the invitation is to a church wedding, the phrase, "request the honour of your presence," is used.

If it is a home, club, or garden wedding or an invitation to a reception use:

"request the pleasure of your company."

Your name must be spelled out in full (no initials), and you must use your middle name, even if you don't like it.

This is also your opportunity to upgrade your social vocabulary. For example, a reception sounds prettier if the invitation reads "Church Fellowship Hall" or "parlour" rather than "Church Basement," though it may very well be the same place.

In listing the wedding date, "Friday, June 14th" bows out in favor of "Friday, the fourteenth of June."

Morning weddings are comparatively rare among Protestants. But they do occur occasionally and quite properly. A reception following a morning wedding is not a "reception" but a "breakfast," even if cake and punch are served. And "morning" means anytime before one o'clock.

The prettier phrases "in the morning" or "in the evening" are used in preference to A.M. and P.M.

How Are the Invitations Worded?

On the following pages are some varied wordings for wedding invitations.

Here is an actual sample.

> Mr. and Mrs. Joseph Steelmann
> request the honour of your presence
> at the marriage of their daughter
> Judith Anne
> to
> Mr. Clarence Leroy Knoll
> Saturday, the eleventh of February
> at half after two o'clock
> Saint Luke's Episcopal Church
> 4865 Holbrook Avenue
> Scranton, Pennsylvania

Other wordings are:

> Mr. and Mrs. Fred Leslie Wilson
> request the honour of your presence
> at the marriage of their daughter
> Audrey Marleen
> to
> Mr. Gary Caldwe'l Brown
> on Friday, the fifth day of June
> nineteen hundred and sixty-four
> at eight o'clock
> First Baptist Church
> Richland, Missouri
> Mr. and Mrs. W. B. Watson
> request the honour of your presence
> at the marriage of their daughter
> Wanda Sue

to
Mr. Jerry R. Warner
on Saturday, the sixth of June
one thousand nine hundred and sixty-four
at seven o'clock in the evening
First Baptist Church
Richland, Missouri

Mr. and Mrs. Howard Stevenson
request the honour of your presence
at the marriage of their daughter
Catherine
to
Mr. John Robert Worthington
Thursday, the second of January
at half after three o'clock
Trinity Church
Phoenix, Arizona

Here are some special sample forms:

If the mother or father is deceased and the living parent has not remarried:

Mrs. Charles Lee Winston
requests the honour of your presence
at the marriage of her daughter
Martha Louise
etc.

or

Mr. Charles Lee Winston
requests the honour of your presence
at the marriage of his daughter
Martha Louise
etc.

If the mother and stepfather issue the invitations:

Mr. and Mrs. Irwin Parker
request the honour of your presence
at the marriage of their daughter
Mary Susan
etc.

If an older married brother issues the invitations:

Mr. and Mrs. John Williams
request the honour of your presence
at the marriage of their sister
Carolyn Joy Williams
etc.

If the older brother is not married:

Mr. John Edward Williams
requests the honour of your presence
at the marriage of his sister
Carolyn Joy Williams
etc.

Grandparents:

Mr. and Mrs. Malcolm Barney Jones
request the honour of your presence
at the marriage of their granddaughter
Marie Evelyn Phillips
etc.

Guardian—when the givers of the wedding are not relatives, the word "Miss" is used with the bride's name:

Mr. and Mrs. Frank Russell
request the honour of your presence
at the marriage of
Miss Penelope Marie Long
etc.

The bride sometimes issues her own invitations:

The honour of your presence
is requested at the marriage of
Miss Elizabeth Ann Stewart
to
Mr. Samuel Paul Simpson
etc.

The invitation to the wedding and to the reception may be combined as:

Mr. and Mrs. Robert Hall
request the honour of your presence
at the marriage of their daughter
Linda Susan
to
Mr. Robert Edward Comstock
on Friday, the twenty-eighth of May
at eight o'clock
First Baptist Church
West Plains, Missouri

Reception
following the ceremony
First Baptist Church

Or, if the guest list is shorter for the reception than for the wedding, you will want to order separate reception cards to include in the invitations to those guests you wish to invite to both the wedding and the reception.

Wedding Breakfast	*Reception*
immediately following the ceremony	*following the ceremony*
Westwood Inn	*First Baptist Church*
1937 Warren Avenue	*Richland, Missouri*
Omaha, Nebraska	

You may also wish to include a response card, sample of which is shown here. The requested response date is usually about ten days before the wedding date.

Please respond
before June ninth

M_____

will _____ *attend*

Quality and Kind of Invitations

You will want to have your invitations engraved on the very best quality paper you can afford. This is the most important invitation ever to be issued in your behalf and you will want it to reflect this fact. Your stationer will show you paper samples of whites and ivories, bond, vellum, or parchment.

He will probably also show you "fashionable" invitations, too. These so-called fashionables are like the plain ones on the inside but are decorated on the outside with wedding bells, rings, hearts, and flowers—or what have you? Some are even bedecked with symbols of Christianity—the Bible, the cross, and the Greek letters alpha and omega. Your stationer may try to sell you these, because that is his business. But they are not generally accepted by etiquette authorities and are not in the best taste today. Anyway, you don't need them.

There will be ample use of the romantic symbols at your prenuptial parties. And as for the Christian symbols, you cannot make your wedding Christian by sending invitations with a golden cross embellished on the cover, any more than you can make your home Christian by hanging a God-Bless-Our-Home plaque on the living room wall! Christianity comes from within and must radiate from your *life,* not from your *belongings.*

The loveliest invitation that you can choose is the traditional white or ivory, conventional fold, engraved in a script reflecting your taste.

The invitation, reception card, and response card are enclosed first in an inner envelope that has no mucilage on the flap and then in an outer envelope which is sealed and addressed.

Invitations are folded with the engraved surface outside. They are inserted, folded edge first, in envelopes with tissue over the engraved surface. The tissue is optional. It is placed there by your engraver to protect the engraving and, if you wish, you may continue to use it after its original function is accomplished.

The invitations are addressed by the bride or her mother (sisters and bridesmaids can help, too) in ink (preferably black) and by hand. They should never be typewritten.

The outside envelope is addressed:

> Mr. and Mrs. John B. Forrester
> 3100 South Jefferson
> Tucumcari, New Mexico

The address on the inner envelope carries the last name only— Mr. and Mrs. Forrester. If Mr. and Mrs. Forrester have young children who are to be invited, the inner envelope reads, Mr. and Mrs. Forrester, Gail, Ellen, and Susan.

As a general rule abbreviations are avoided. The exceptions are long established contractions such as Mr., Mrs., or Jr. House numbers are written in figures. Street names which are numbers are usually written out, as 1587 Seventh Street. The correct social title for a man, either the bridegroom or the one issuing the invitations is "Mr." with the exceptions of: Reverend, Doctor, Judge, Justice and titles of military officers. Letters of degrees are never used. The military has a protocol all its own, governed by rank. For example, noncommissioned officers and enlisted men in the Army, Air Force, and Marine Corps, Charles David Bunch, United States Army; lieutenants, Charles David Bunch, Lieutenant, United States Army; captains and higher, Captain Charles David Bunch, United States Army.

Naval petty officers and seamen are addressed: Charles David Bunch, United States Navy; ensigns and higher, Charles David Bunch, Ensign, United States Navy; commander or higher, Commodore Charles David Bunch, United States Navy.

The post office prefers that the return address be handwritten on the upper left hand corner of the outside envelope. It is socially correct, also. Or, if you prefer, the return address may be *embossed* on the back outside envelope flap.

Invitations should be mailed approximately three weeks before the date of the wedding. If, however, you are having a Christmas wedding, and if you think your invitations might be lost in the Christmas rush, you might mail them a little earlier. And, of course, they are always sent first class.

Stationery Accessories

When you order your invitations you may want to order matching accessories, such as informal thank-you cards—a folded card with the name or initials of the bride (before the wedding) or the married name of the couple (after the wedding) engraved on the front. The inside may be used by the bride to write her own personal thank-you notes.

Reception cards, response cards and envelopes; social stationery; napkins; place cards for the wedding breakfast or dinner; and pew cards, if needed, should also be ordered.

Pew cards should be mailed with invitations to special people. The people receiving these cards simply present them to an usher. Some pew cards are specifically numbered, some merely say "behind the ribbons" or "within the ribbons" (as the case may be). Whatever they say, this system surely works a lot better than the one that depends on the head usher to recognize and properly seat all these people. He might be performing another important function, like smiling at a bridesmaid, when dear great Aunt Penelope arrives and he might miss her. Alas, Aunt Penelope will never be the same should she be incorrectly pewed.

Your stationery dealer will show you printed thank you's, but please do not order any. A thank you is not a thank you unless it is your own thank you!

Wedding Announcements

It used to be customary to order wedding invitations for those close enough to attend, and wedding announcements for those too far away to attend. Now, as a simple means of advising them that the wedding is to take place, it has become perfectly acceptable to send invitations to those friends too far to come. A wedding invitation does not call for a gift unless a reception invitation is included, but some of your faraway friends and family will want to send gifts anyway.

The announcement is now generally used when a wedding is to be very small or private. It is mailed after the ceremony, preferably the same day. Sometimes "At-Home" cards, are enclosed to let friends know your new address.

I hope that you will never need this advice, but should it become necessary to postpone the wedding the proper form, which should also be engraved, is:

Mr. and Mrs. Lynn Forest Johnson
announce that the marriage of their daughter
Suzanne
to
Mr. Kenneth Howard Thompson
has been postponed
from
Friday, the eighth of May
until
Friday, the third of June
at four o'clock
First Presbyterian Church
Joplin

You do not give the reason for the postponement. Don't forget to notify the newspaper, too.

Should your engagement be broken after your invitations have been mailed, and if there is time before the announced date, send out engraved notices withdrawing the wedding invitations.

Mr. and Mrs. Delmar Paul Kessinger
announce that the marriage of their daughter
Cynthia Elizabeth
to
Mr. Thomas Anthony Cook
will not take place.

Again, no reason must be given, no excuses made—and do not spend a lot of time brooding about it. If circumstances have altered your plans, it is much better *this* side of the altar than later. You will, in time, recover; and, the less talking and thinking you do about it, the quicker the recovery!

7

Select the *Right* Music

The selection of good music and good musicians is of primary importance to the beauty of your wedding. Both the music and the musicians should be given at least as much consideration as the style of your wedding gown. The sound of music, more than any other one element of your wedding, will create the atmosphere you desire and virtually establish the "personality" of the wedding.

Be traditional, if you please, but don't be a copycat! Do not choose music for your wedding just because you have heard it at every wedding you've attended. There is no excuse for having music that is "blah." Select music that is YOU!

Some churches have established policies both as to whom the musicians may be and what music may be used. But most churches leave the choices to the bride with guidance from her minister or minister of music.

Choose musicians who are capable. Wedding music, as a whole, is difficult to play and sing. A faltering musician, whether an organist or vocalist, will create a tenseness among the wedding guests and, perhaps, even among the wedding party (if they are close enough to hear). I do not mean to imply that you should import professionals from the Metropolitan Opera, but rather to insist that you make your choice among musicians whom you personally know to be very capable. A solo is usually (though *not* necessarily)

one of the first items in the order of a wedding service, and I've seen
many weddings almost spoiled by a frightened, timid soloist who
has been prevailed upon by some close friend to "please sing at my
wedding." This is not the place to use a close friend who sings an
occasional solo in church. Use *that* friend somewhere else in the
wedding party.

There is no law, written or unwritten, that declares that wedding
music must be sung nor that it must be by a soloist. Vocal duets
(a happily married couple perhaps), piano and organ arrangements, or violin and piano arrangements blend perfectly into the
reverent spell inspired by the candlelit sanctuary.

At one of the loveliest weddings my husband ever performed
there was no vocal music at all. The entire music was beautifully
played on the pipe organ.

There are two schools of thought among ministers as to what
music is actually appropriate for the wedding service.

The first group maintains that because the wedding is a religious
ceremony, a divine ordinance, and a form of worship, all of the
music must be sacred—of church origin. At a wedding planned
under the guidance of a minister in this group, a program such as
this might be followed:

Organ Prelude—	selected hymns	
Possible	*Praise Ye the Father*	Gounod
Processionals—	*Festival March*	Gounod
	March Romaine	Gounod
	Joyful, Joyful, We Adore Thee	Beethoven
Possible	*O Perfect Love*	Barnby
Vocal Solos—	*The Voice That Breathed O'er Eden*	Keble-Dykes
	Song of Ruth	Singer
	The Wedding Prayer	Dunlap
	The Lord's Prayer	Malotte
Possible	*Blest Be the Tie*	Nageli
Instrumental	*Saviour, Like a Shepherd Lead Us*	Bradbury
Solos—	*O Jesus, I Have Promised*	
	O Master, Let Me Walk with Thee	Smith
	O Love That Will Not Let Me Go	Herbert
Recessional—	*Doxology* (from the *German Psalter*)	

Such a selection of wedding music would certainly emphasize the spiritual aspect of the occasion and would create a beautiful, worshipful atmosphere.

Let me caution you to be exceedingly careful in choosing the hymns. It goes without saying that certain hymns and gospel songs, while beautiful in their places, do not belong in wedding ceremonies. We have all heard the timeworn jokes about using "The Strife Is O'er" or "When the Battle's Over." But there are many, many other songs which I feel are inappropriate for weddings. Unfortunately, some of these have occasionally, and with the best of intentions, found their way into wedding services. Perhaps the most startling example of this occurred at a wedding we attended some years ago.

It was a thrilling moment in the wedding processional when the bride, arrayed in white splendor, began her walk down the aisle. Suddenly the music of the processional was silent, and the bride stopped. All eyes and ears shifted to the groom who, while standing at the altar, sang to the bride, "I'd Rather Have Jesus!" I'm sure the couple planned this in an effort to impress upon the congregation their good intent to put the Lord first in their marriage, but it somehow just didn't have that effect on the guests.

Some songs which are appropriate as instrumental solos are not suitable for vocal solos.

"Blest Be the Tie" IS about love, but it is about the agape or godly kind of love, not the love of man for woman; and anyway the words are a bit remorseful. They speak of "woes," "burdens," "sympathizing tears," "parting," and "inward pain"—all of which may actually become a part of the marriage that is being solemnized. But let's not emphasize THAT side of marriage at the wedding by using "Blest Be the Tie" as a vocal solo. If you must, use it in the organ prelude, as a candle-lighting number, or as a background for a prayer. Somehow we do not get the idea of great sadness when we hear it instrumentally.

Similarly, the words of "Saviour, Like a Shepherd Lead Us," "O Jesus, I Have Promised," and dozens of other lovely hymns in this category were written—and beautifully so—about the *Christian* life, not the *marital* life. While some phrases of these songs very definitely apply to all phases of Christian life, including marriage, others just do not.

I mean to cast no reflection whatever on these hymns. But, while they do lift our hearts as a part of worship services, they were not written for weddings.

Then there are songs that are sacred to some people but not to others. Schubert's "Ave Maria," for example, is a beautiful musical composition, but "Ave Maria" means "Hail, Mary" and is, in fact, a prayer of a young girl to the virgin Mary. I cannot think of any circumstance that would make this song appropriate at a Protestant wedding.

The second school of clerical thought includes those ministers who feel that although certain songs were not of divinely inspired origin, they have become appropriate through constant *usage* at weddings. These ministers are aware that songs like "Because" and "I Love Thee" are bride-centered, not God-centered, but they maintain that many other facets of the ceremony are bride-centered —the aisle cloth, the sprinkling of the flower petals in the path the bride will walk, the custom of the guests' standing in honor of the bride, and even the "to love and to cherish" part of the ceremony. A wedding service is a worship experience, but it is a special one, making it possible for the bride and groom to declare in "the presence of God and these witnesses" their love *for each other,* as well as their love for God.

These clergymen would, therefore, endorse wedding music of this nature:

Organ Prelude	*Clair de Lune*	Debussy
	Remembrance	Davies
	On Wings of Song	Mendelssohn
	A Shepherd's Tale	Nevin
	Flower Song	Lange
	Love's Greeting	Elgar
	Liebestraum	Liszt

	Lo, Now a Rose Appeareth	Kreckel
	Air	Bach
	God's Time Is Best	Bach
	Jesu, Joy of Man's Desiring	Bach
	Salut d'Amour	Diggle
	La Serenata	Braga
	Consolation	Mendelssohn
Entrance of the Wedding Party—	*Pas Des Bouquetieres* *(March of the Flower Girls)*	Wachs
Entrance of the Bride—	*Bridal Chorus* from Lohengrin	Wagner
Vocal Solos	*Trumpet Tune*	Purcell
	Because	D'Hardelot
	Always	Berlin
	O Promise Me	De Koven
	I Love Thee	Grieg
	I Love You Truly	Bond
	If I Could Tell You	Firestone
Recessional	*Wedding March* from *Midsummer Night's Dream*	Mendelssohn
	Chaconne	Couperin

Do not misunderstand. This is not an effort to list all appropriate wedding songs in either sacred or secular categories. It is just to give you an idea of the type music to be considered.

Again, let me admonish you to let good taste be your guide. The words of many secular love songs are more uncomfortable in church than Goldilocks was in Papa Bear's chair. Some are too meaningless and hackneyed. Some are too sensuous. A love ballad written for guitar accompaniment almost never adapts itself willingly to organ or piano. And then, some songs, such as the beautiful "Autumn Leaves," are far too melancholic for a wedding. Just like "Blest Be the Tie" is about separation, "Autumn Leaves" is completely irrelevant to the marriage service.

You should personally examine every phrase of each song you think you want used in your wedding service. Ask yourself, "Does this really declare musically what I want expressed?" Then, "Is this song really appropriate for my Christian wedding?"

While I heartily recommend the all-sacred music wedding (with the exception of the traditional processional and recessional, which I personally prefer) as being the loveliest of all weddings, I can understand the thinking of those pastors who feel that *usage* rather than *origin* is the criterion for worshipful music. Our grandparents loved the song "When the Saints Go Marching In" and it was used often as a part of the long-ago worship service. Today, it is a rare occasion when we hear it in our churches. Why? Because *usage* by jazz musicians has, unfortunately, lifted it from its original intent and placed it in an entirely different light in the world of music. It seems to me no less a transformation than this that "Bridal Chorus," originally written for opera, has become such an integral part of the wedding service. And, I am most anxious to see in the years to come what will happen to the lovely prayer song "One Hand, One Heart," from the musical *West Side Story*. It has already found its way into weddings in this area. I predict that some day its origin will be forgotten and that it will be thought of in the same light as "Because" is today—purely weddingish!

Whether secular or sacred, the choice is yours, so long as it is within the policy framework of your church and meets the approval of your minister.

If you find that your church disapproves all music of secular association, and if you are disappointed because you will not be able to use your favorite song or that special melody which you think of as *our* song, let me suggest to both you and your minister this compromise. Use the all-sacred music in the sanctuary as a part of the ceremony. Then, at the reception, provide a piano background, or even a piano-violin background of romantic wedding music which will add to the festiveness of the occasion. "My Best to You" by Isham Jones might be suitable during the cutting of the cake. The song that brought you together might be sung just prior to the throwing of the bridal bouquet.

Some ministers approve a very quiet musical background throughout the ceremony. This can be sweet if it is not too loud.

If you choose a song which has a very familiar refrain but an unfamiliar verse, it is up to you to decide whether you want the complete song or only the part which is most familiar.

At neither the wedding nor the reception should the groom sing to the bride or the bride sing to the groom, unless they are professional vocalists who are *never* nervous, have *never* suffered stage fright, and *all* the guests are unnervous people. Express your love for each other with frequent smiles but NOT with music. If you just must sing to each other, there'll be time for it while you are driving to your honeymoon hideaway—if you still feel so inclined.

One last word about music. Our own church organist uses the organ chimes to count out the hour of the wedding. If an eight o'clock wedding is planned, precisely at that hour, when everything is in order and the bride's mother has been seated, the organist plays eight chimes, like the chiming of a beautiful clock, and it becomes a signal to the guests that the lovely hour has come at last.

8
Showers, Parties, and Teas

There's going to be a party and it's in *your* honor. In fact, there are likely to be several parties and you will be the guest of honor at all of them. Your friends will plan wonderful showers for you. They will spend money unselfishly on refreshments, napkins, nuts, mints, flowers, favors. They may even devote long hours of their time to fashioning frilly decorations and lacy nut cups. They will buy for *you* lamps and linens, china and chintz, rugs and recipe books—things they long for but think they can't afford for themselves—all because they love you and they are happy that you are to be married. This is their way of sharing your joy.

I hope that as you read the last paragraph you smiled an old-fashioned "Oh, Goody!" little girl type smile, because if you did, it is a sure sign that you will be a beautiful bride. Beauty is in the eye of the beholder, and though your friends are willing to go all out to shower you with gifts, they do expect, and rightfully so, a genuine graciousness and a sincerely expressed gratitude. If you do not know how to express gratitude, learn it now. Stand in front of your mirror for five minutes each day and say to your image, "Oh, thank you!" until the girl on the other side of the mirror convinces you that she means it.

Now, to the specifics.

Who Will Shower You?

Your friends!—The best showers are given by your close friends, perhaps your maid of honor, your bridesmaids, or your mother's friends. Someday soon a friend will call you and say, "I'm planning to give a shower for you." This is your very first opportunity to be a gracious bride-to-be. Say, "Oh, thank you! That would be so nice!"—and *mean* it.

Your relatives.—A bridal shower should never be given by either a member of your family or the groom's family. There are other prenuptial parties they may give, but under no circumstances should these close family members extend invitations to any kind of wedding party requiring the bringing of a gift. Perhaps you have a doting aunt who will help you arrange and pay for your bridesmaids' luncheon, or even your wedding reception. This is fine, provided she thinks of it, not you, and provided it meets the approval of your parents. Or, perhaps the groom has an older brother who wants to help plan and finance the rehearsal dinner. The same rules apply to the relatives of the groom.

One lovely aunt I know, who wanted to do something special for her nephew's bride-to-be, planned a sewing party. The invitations, which were extended to the women of the wedding party and to close relatives, read, "You're invited to a *party* in honor of Mary" (not *shower*). At the party each guest was provided a stamped kitchen towel, embroidery thread, needle, thimble, and hoops—all of the materials necessary to complete the towels—and the activities for the afternoon included sewing and talking. The happy, bride-centered conversation accompanying the work ruled out any need for entertainment and made the occasion a joyous affair. Just before refreshments were served, the finished towels (complete with embroidered initials of their creators) were presented to the bride, who now remembers that happy afternoon every time she uses one.

Churches and church organizations.—There is only one type of completely successful church-sponsored shower that I know about, and that is the wedding shower given by a rural church where the spiritual and social life of its members are so thoroughly blended that they cannot be completely separated. This is the kind of shower that the whole community is enthusiastic about.

The bride and groom are both guests of honor and the men, as well as the women, attend. Most gifts are presented jointly to the couple, but there are always some things, such as a sewing kit or a recipe book, just for the bride. And the groom receives tools or fishing gear or good books to start his library. Someone invariably brings a fun gift—a rolling pin for the bride, or a can opener for the groom. No one need worry a great deal about entertainment at the rural church shower, for the entertainment for these salt-of-the-earth people is just being together to enjoy good old-fashioned visiting. Refreshments, fresh out of the ovens of the women of the church, are always both plentiful and delectable.

Unfortunately, this custom does not carry over too well to the small town and big city churches where the social life of the members is, for the most part, separated from church activities. Unless you have the good fortune to belong to a lovely little country church where showering is an established successful custom, it is better to say, "No thank you," to the church or church organization offering to shower you. If you are not a faithful member, guests will not *come* because you haven't *gone*. And, alas, if you are a faithful member, guests are inclined not to come because they think "there will be such a crowd they won't miss me."

If this should puzzle or disappoint you, reflect for a moment on this thought. It is not really one of the functions of the church of the living God to entertain socially, and a wedding shower is a purely social event. Your church will assist you in many other ways connected with your wedding. It will provide the minister, the altar, and the music. Your pastor will give advice concerning all of your wedding plans and especially concerning the establishment of your Christian home. This is the important role the church should take to help you with your wedding preparations, because this is the *spiritual* "till death do us part" side of your marriage.

The showers, lovely and wonderful as they may be, are the material extras in wedding preliminaries.

So, if you can possibly manipulate it, leave the showering festivities in the hands of your friends rather than churches or organizations. No matter how amateur they may be at giving showers, friends function much better than the best of appointed committees.

As to every rule, there is at least one exception. The one *I'm* thinking of is the bride-to-be who lives in the parsonage—the minister's daughter. When a member of the pastor's family marries, all of the members of the church not only want to be invited to a shower, they *expect* to be. Blessed is the bride who has grown up in the midst of a congregation of people who love her. The entire parish thinks of her as "our bride" and the parishioners are lavish in the giving of good gifts to her. She opens present after present after present, each one lovelier than the last. Suddenly she forgets that she has ever complained about her fishbowl existence. The windows of heaven are open and are pouring out blessings upon her! The daughters of the wealthy seldom receive more lavish showers than do the daughters of the clergy!

When Shall the Showers Be?

Hostesses will check with you about possible dates. Showers usually begin about six weeks before the wedding, and it is best not to schedule any within the week immediately preceding the wedding date. You and your wedding party will be busy by that time with other wedding preparations.

Some hostesses (thank goodness, not many) like to surprise the bride-to-be. Whether you like surprises or not, you are likely to be surprised with some type of prenuptial shower. So let me caution you, never go anywhere during the two months preceding your wedding unless you look your best. And, if a friend should call and say, "Come over for a few minutes. Don't bother to dress. Just come as you are," beware! Take those rollers out of your hair, get out of those slacks, and put on a neat (but not too party-ish) dress. Then when you arrive and a room full of your friends welcome you with shouts of "Surprise, Surprise!" go the second mile. Be especially gracious by *being* surprised and pleased. They'll love you for it.

What Kind of Showers Will You Have?

Occasionally a hostess will ask what kind of shower you need or prefer. You are free to make suggestions, provided they *are* suggestions and not requests. Usually, though, by the time a hostess contacts you she has a definite plan in mind. The number and kinds of showers you will be given will be limited only by the imagination of your friends.

Here are a few of the "usuals":

The general (or miscellaneous) shower.—This is the all-inclusive shower where the opening of each white-tissued, silver-ribboned package is a lovely surprise. You may receive anything from a fitted picnic basket and thermos jug set to a pair of hand-carved bookends or an electric steam or dry iron. Some people give practical gifts and some frivolous. *I* always choose something that I would like to have for myself. If your friends plan one large shower for you, rather than several small ones, this is the kind of shower you will probably have.

A kitchen shower.—Gifts are all concentrated on your future kitchen. They may include cutlery, canisters, cookware, cookbooks, dish towels, potholders, or even small appliances such as toasters, mixers, coffeemakers, electric skillets, or knife sharpeners.

Know your color scheme and tell the hostess.

A recipe shower.—Guests bring their favorite recipes and the ingredients for making them. For example, a bridesmaid, who couldn't care less about cooking, arrives with a box of corn bread mix, a spatula for mixing it, and a pan for baking it—all beautifully gift wrapped, and for you. The hostess usually furnishes the bulky staples, such as flour, shortening, and sugar. She must coordinate the planning so that all do not bring recipes for the same meat potpie. One guest may indicate to the hostess that she is bringing a salad recipe, another a cake, another a pie, another a macaroni casserole.

After the foods are prepared, the hostess will file the recipes in a card file or a loose-leaf notebook (there are several nice ones out now with decorative covers and appropriate dividers), which she will present to you.

A pantry shower.—This one is a carryover from the old New England custom of "pounding" newlyweds. Each guest brings a "pound" of something for your pantry: canned vegetables and fruits, canned meats, cocoa, baking soda, powdered sugar, vanilla, nutmeats, and on and on through all the items on all the shelves of your nearest supermarket.

A linen shower.—"Linen" does not, for some peculiar reason, mean items made from the cloth of the thread of the flax plant. I do not understand why, but I'm glad it doesn't, because you will be grateful to receive towels, washcloths, bath mats, and bedspreads made of cotton or synthetic materials, blankets of luxurious yarn, table cloths of linen or cotton or lace—in short, anything that might be found in your future linen closet.

A personal shower.—Close friends usually give this one, because knowledge of your correct size and personal taste is much more important here. Gifts include filmy items of personal lingerie—dreamy gowns, robes, slippers, dusters, shifts; fresh and gleaming new handkerchiefs and gloves. Hosiery belongs in this category and so does costume jewelry. Beauty aids, such as perfumes, powders, bath oils, lotions, and colognes are good. Perhaps someone will think to give you a purse-size New Testament or a small book of devotionals.

The anniversary shower.—This type of shower will be given by a hostess who likes a good theme to tie together decorations, entertainment, and refreshments. A dozen guests may be invited and encouraged to bring gifts representing the wedding anniversaries. That is, the guest choosing the first anniversary would bring a gift of paper. The guest choosing the second anniversary would bring a gift of cotton, and so on. Here is the complete list:

First	Paper
Second	Cotton
Third	Leather
Fourth	Fruit, Flowers
Fifth	Wood
Sixth	Candy
Seventh	Wool, Copper
Eighth	Bronze, Pottery
Ninth	Pottery, Willow
Tenth	Tin
Eleventh	Steel
Twelfth	Silk, Linen
Thirteenth	Lace
Fourteenth	Ivory
Fifteenth	Crystal
Twentieth	China
Twenty-fifth	Silver
Thirtieth	Pearl
Thirty-fifth	Coral
Fortieth	Ruby
Forty-fifth	Sapphire
Fiftieth	Golden
Fifty-fifth	Emerald
Seventy-fifth	Diamond

I have given the whole list, but I really think that after the fifteenth maybe, and certainly after the twenty-fifth, the material symbol is too elaborate for shower-giving.

Probably the most important thing to remember about all of these shower ideas is, don't take them too seriously! Sometimes people get so wrapped up trying to take exactly the right gift to the right shower, or the bride herself gets so involved with categorizing her gifts, that the *fun* part of the shower almost disappears. Relax and enjoy your showers. You will remember that bridesmaid and her box of cornbread mix long after you have forgotten the proper gifts brought to that shower by proper people. It's little things like this that make up your wedding memories—that make your pre-nuptial parties and your wedding itself different from everyone else's.

What Manner Showers?

The manner in which your showers will be given is also almost limitless. You should be familiar with some of the showering methods.

The party shower.—A shower may be a party at which games are played and favors given. Should the games be of the contest variety and should prizes be awarded guests, custom usually dictates that the winning guest pass along her prize to the bride. The thoughtful hostess will meet this situation graciously by providing identical prizes—one for the winner and one for the bride.

Presents at this type shower are usually arranged on a table and are opened by the bride-to-be as the climax to all other festivities of the evening. Opened presents are either passed around so that guests may examine them or they are displayed where the guests may see them before or after refreshments are served.

The luncheon shower.—Often a bride-to-be is honored at a luncheon given by her bridesmaids and close friends. She is usually presented a corsage and a gift from the hostesses and a collective gift from the other guests. This is probably because of the transportation and handling problems that would result if many bulky gifts were brought, particularly if the luncheon is held in a restaurant or private club. Gifts are sometimes brought by all the guests, however. The hostesses might specify that the gifts be pieces of table silver or personal shower items.

The joint shower.—Now growing in popularity is the joint shower, one which includes the groom! This is fun, because the groom shares in the excitement of opening presents and he gets a firsthand look at them. The joint shower is almost always an evening event so that the friends of the groom can also be invited. I have been to a few unhappy showers where the groom was present and helped open the gifts, but without much enjoyment, because he was the only man present! I hope no hostess will place your groom in this unhappy situation.

The open house shower.—Another shower may take the form of

an open house or a tea, with the bride opening each gift as it is
presented and guests being served as they arrive. Entertainment at
this type shower is usually conversation. A good hostess will have
several assistants to see that conversation in all of the entertaining
rooms is kept going and that all guests are included in it.

What Manners the Bride?

On registering preferences.—So that your china pieces will all be
of the same pattern there are many people who want to know what
pattern you prefer. You may, therefore, register your preference
for china, silver, and crystal patterns at a jewelry or department
store or bridal gift shop. Do not offer the information that you
have done this unless you are specifically asked by a hostess or by
someone invited to a shower. Even then, be exceedingly tactful so
that you don't leave the impression that you absolutely must have a
specific gift.

On showers in general.—Arrive promptly at the hour expressed
by your hostess (probably half an hour earlier than the guests
arrive).

Your hostess will ask you to select two or three friends to assist
with the opening of your gifts. One helper usually makes a list of
the gifts and donors so that the thank-you notes will be accurately
written. You may buy beautifully bound wedding gift record books
for this purpose. Some include numbers in gummed sticker form
which your helper may affix to the gift almost as soon as you have
opened it. This is certainly the best way to maintain an accurate
gift record. The same book is used for all showers and for the
wedding gifts with the numbers running consecutively in the order
the gifts are received.

Another helper tries to maintain some semblance of order among
the gift wrappings and ribbons. Most brides discard the wrappings
but keep the bows. Even when the wrapping paper is to be discarded it must be folded neatly and boxed, or you will find yourself
sitting in a rumpled mountain of it before you have opened all of
your gifts.

Occasionally a situation exists where a bride-to-be does not know all of the people invited to her showers. Guests may be friends of the groom's family. This is particularly true when the bride and groom do not live in the same town or share the same church or college. In this case, it is a good idea for the shower honoree to choose as one of her helpers someone who does know everyone who will be present at the shower. (Your hostess can suggest someone.) This assistant can help you relate gift to giver and you will not only have the pleasure of receiving the gift but also the joy of making a new friend.

On the fine art of gratitude.—Express appreciation the minute you open a gift. If the giver is present at the shower, try to let your eyes meet hers with a look of gratitude. And say, "Thank you"; "Oh, how lovely!"; "Just what I hoped it would be!"; "How very nice!"; "What a thoughtful gift!" or one of your own joyous phrases. Do NOT merely hold up a gift into which someone has poured time and money and announce flatly, "This is from the Smiths." If you can't do better than that, don't let anyone give a shower for you!

Gushiness is not a very desirable character trait, but if you cannot express gratitude without it, then learn to gush a little. You do not have to be hypocritical and say, "Oh, Aunt Tillie, I adore purple towels! when your planned bathroom is tangerine. But DO say something honest and sincere. How about, "Thank you, Aunt Tillie. My! How soft these towels are!" Time changes tastes. Your next apartment may have a lavender powder room. Don't make the mistake of thinking of that first apartment as your forever-after. It is only your first home, and many gifts which will not fit into that first apartment may prove later to be the most useful.

Thank the guests again as they are leaving the shower. Try to concentrate on who gave what as you open the gifts so that you can make this parting thank you a genuine one. If you just can't remember the specific gift, at least muster up something like, "Thank you so much for coming. It was a wonderful shower. I'm so excited I can hardly wait to look at all the gifts again!"

Each shower gift and each wedding gift must be acknowledged
with a handwritten thank-you note. Commercially printed thank-
you notes will not do. I'm going to be a bit radical here and suggest
that you write your thank-you letters on the *same* night as the
shower. You're too excited to sleep anyway. You are still envel-
oped in the thrill of receiving the gifts. And you've certainly
burned midnight oil for a lot less important things than expressing
gratitude. If you just can't write them the same night, at least do it
the next day. Get your thank-you's in the mail as soon as possible
after a shower. Your friends will be both delighted and surprised
to receive them.

A thank-you letter need not be long, but it must be personal.
For example:

> DEAR MRS. FARMER:
>
> Thank you so much for the lovely
> linen tablecloth and matching napkins.
> It is just the perfect background for
> our china. I'm sure you must have
> thought of this when you selected it
> for us, and I appreciate your thought-
> fulness very much.
>
> Sincerely,
>
> JEAN JONES

Or, it could take a form like this:

> DEAR SALLY,
> Thank you for sharing with me your
> recipe for tomato aspic. How many times
> Jim has enjoyed eating it at your house!
> And how nice of you to provide the in-
> gredients. What a joy it will be to move
> into our apartment with already stocked
> cabinets!
>
> Affectionately,
> JEAN

Shower thank-you's are to be written on a good quality plain or engraved note paper. If the paper is imprinted, it should carry the bride's initials only and should not say, "Jim and I appreciate." However, I personally think it is nice to work Jim in, especially when a gift has come from his family, friends, or relatives. This can be done even on prewedding thank-you's. For example:

> DEAR MRS. YOUNG,
>
> Thank you for the beautiful hand-made walnut salad set. The grain of the wood is so lovely. Jim came this morning to see all the gifts, and he was especially pleased with your selection. We are both delighted.
>
> Lovingly,
>
> JEAN JONES

Most modern authorities declare that a shower gift thank-you letter should be directed only to a woman, with perhaps one sentence tacked on asking that woman to "please express my appreciation to Mr. Dustin, too." This strikes me as being a peculiar and unnecessary custom—peculiar because Mr. Dustin probably paid for the gift and unnecessary because when a gift enclosure card has been signed by both husband and wife, it seems so much more logical to simply address your thank-you letter to the couple.

But, if you are more concerned about etiquette than logic, here is the accepted form:

> DEAR MRS. JOHNSON:
>
> I am so pleased with the lovely punch bowl. You must have known how much I like milk glass.
>
> Please express my gratitude to Mr. Johnson, too.
>
> Sincerely,
>
> JEAN JONES

If a gift must be returned, a tactful thank-you note can ease the giver's pain, like this:

> DEAR MRS. ROAM,
>
> How nice it was of you to suggest that we return the pretty alarm clock which you selected for us, but which was duplicated. We followed your suggestion to exchange it for a kitchen clock. So now you will still help us number our hours, and we'll not only be up on time, we'll have meals on time!
>
> I appreciate your extra thoughtfulness.
>
> JEAN JONES

It is better not to exchange gifts unless the giver makes it a point of insistence. It is much better to keep pairs of gifts and express sincere gratitude for each than to hurt the feelings of either giver.

Then there are gifts that are more special than others by virtue of the amount of time expended to make them, or the amount of money spent for them. The givers of these special gifts should receive special thank-you's like this:

> DEAR MRS. BURD,
>
> I am simply overwhelmed with the beautiful Williamsburg bedspread you made for us. So many cross-stitches! It must have taken you years of work. Be assured that we shall treasure this work of art and that we will think of you and your generosity every time we look at it!
>
> Lovingly,
>
> BETTY WRIGHT

A Christian bride should be especially grateful and should *express* her gratitude clearly and promptly. Some brief rules to remember are:

1. Call the gift by name.
2. Tell some specific reason why you are glad to have *that* gift.
3. Don't just acknowledge receipt of a gift. Express gratitude for it.

And, don't get carried away religiously and use Scripture verses to express your gratitude. Scripture verses, like the printed thank-you cards, are not originals with you, and, therefore, are not good thank-you's. Besides, it takes a real theologian to find appropriate ones.

One more thing. . . . Now that you've written those shower thank-you's early, just like I told you to, and you're on your way to the post office and you bump right into Miss McFarland who gave you an electric French bread warmer, and to whom you have written a note, do you:

———— mutter "G'mornin' " to her and hurry on your way?

———— fumble through the envelopes until you come to hers, hand it to her and declare excitedly, "You've just saved me a nickel!"

———— make small talk with her about the weather and the high school football game . . . not mentioning the shower?

No, of course not. None of these.

That written thank-you letter is not the sum total of your gratefulness. It is only the outward expression of the inward gratitude you feel. So, when you see Miss McFarland, you will want to exclaim, "Oh, Miss McFarland, thank you for the wonderful French bread warmer. I just love that red and white checked cover. It will certainly add atmosphere to our spaghetti suppers. I was just thrilled with the shower! I appreciate it so much." Then on with the weather and football game talk and the mailing of the written thank-you's.

In addition to shower gifts, you will receive wedding gifts. The general rule is that persons accepting invitations to the wedding AND reception are to respond with a wedding gift. But custom varies from place to place and in many areas the same persons do not give both elaborate shower gifts and elaborate wedding gifts. The shower gift may be quite small and the wedding gift of more consequence, or a donor may choose one lovely gift and present it as either a shower or wedding gift. Don't expect several gifts from the same person, but be especially grateful if you do get more than one. Don't wait to write a thank-you letter because you think "she might give me something else, too." *She* might not, and your thank-you would be tardy!

Wedding gift thank-you letters differ from shower thank-you's in that they can be written a few at a time as the gifts come in. In this case, bridal stationery is used and the note is written by the bride over her signature. Or, they may be written after the wedding (if not too much time has elapsed) on the couple's new stationery and signed "Jim and Mary."

Your mother and the mother of the groom are almost always invited to shower festivities. They are not required to bring gifts (though they sometimes do). Your parents will buy you the nicest wedding present they can afford. They will probably ask you what you would like most. In *this* case, tell them. Custom was that silver and china were the parental gift items. But now that gift is just as likely to be a portable TV or an automatic washer. Whatever it is, when you have moved into your new home and are a bit settled, sit down and write the most important thank-you letters of all— one to your new in-laws, thanking them for their wedding gift and for all the help they gave to make your wedding a lovely one; and one to your own dear parents, thanking them for the wedding gift and for the gift of the wedding itself.

Do not forget to include among your thank-you letters those to the hostesses who planned and gave the showers for you. Write the thank-you's. Make them your very own and let them radiate *your* thankfulness.

Above all, don't get so involved with your gift treasures that you lose sight of yourself. There may be many times you will not be able to use that ivory-handled steak knife set, because you can't afford to buy steak. At first, you may not even have a dining room table to show off that imported cutwork cloth. It is a rough transition from a few weeks of having *everything* new to an unaccustomed life of saving money for perhaps months to buy *one* thing new.

It is somewhat of a shock to move out of your parents' well-equipped home, where years of accumulation have left little to be desired, into a small and sparsely furnished apartment. It is almost like Cinderella's chariot turning into a pumpkin. But a lovely pumpkin it is, because it is your very own. Be grateful for the beginning things and patient enough to wait for the rest. Know that more important than any material possession is a sweet, unselfish, unspoiled YOU, for the very loveliest treasure you can take to that new apartment is YOU.

9

To Honor Your Guests

All of the prewedding festivities are not bride-centered. Some of the parties are designed for the entertainment of other members of the wedding party, the givers of presents, the out-of-town guests, and the families.

The Bridesmaids' Luncheon

This luncheon is customarily given by the bride for her bridesmaids. Specifically you can include all female members of the wedding party, or you can limit the guest list to those who are having special dresses made for the occasion. Plan to have it after a gown-fitting excursion, and even call it a "Bridesmaids' *Fitting* Luncheon" (carrying out a theme at the luncheon of needles, thread, and thimbles, place cards shaped like pieces of patterns, and so on), so that the other women will not feel left out. Other authorities say you may or may not invite your mother-in-law to be. I say, by all means, invite her—and, of course, your own mother.

Etiquette books are full of things that you have a *right* to do or not to do. If you are not in the mood for company, they say, you can send your parlor maid to the door to say, "Madam isn't receiving guests this afternoon." Well, if the caller is a normal person with normal reactions, she will probably hum a "ta-te-ta," shake the dust from her feet, and you won't be receiving her as a guest the next afternoon or the next either. Surely these bits of advice were not written for Christians. At any rate they should not be adhered to by the people who sing, "Others, Lord, yes, *others*." No wonder the world is full of skeptics who accuse Christians of "straining at gnats and swallowing camels!"

Make sure your groom's mother is invited. And be certain also that she has a wonderful time. Happy and lasting relationships are built on small but solid foundations.

Though this luncheon is the bride's responsibility, it is especially thoughtful if an aunt or friend offers to hostess this party. It may be in a home, a club, hotel, restaurant, or tearoom.

No matter where it is, the hostess will want to personally supervise the decorating and setting of the tables. The floral centerpiece can be very feminine, and there should be place cards, special napkins, and the prettiest table service available. Perhaps you will want to use as a background for the table service and centerpiece a lovely linen cloth in the same color as the bridesmaids' dresses for the wedding.

Invitations are usually extended by phone, but if it is to be a very large bridesmaids' luncheon, invitations may be written *by hand* on informals, using this pattern:

> *Mrs. Dwight Burg*
> *requests the pleasure of your company*
> *at a bridesmaids' luncheon*
> *on Saturday, the tenth of May*
> *at one o'clock*
> *Hickory Hills Country Club*

R.S.V.P.
915 East Elm

You may wish to present gifts to your attendants at this time, though I think it is better to wait until the rehearsal dinner.

One nice old tradition that you may wish to follow at this party is the serving of a cake into which has been baked (carefully wrapped in foil) a quantity of items with symbolic meaning to the bridesmaids who find them within their slices of cake:

A dime stands for riches.

A ring means she'll be next to wed.

A thimble.—Oh, dear! She'll be an old maid!

A wishbone means she'll have lots of luck.

A tiny boat.—In her future a long voyage.

A miniature boy doll.—Romance is in store.

A miniature animal.—She'll marry a farmer.

A miniature stethoscope.—She'll marry Ben Casey!

After the fun and the luncheon, it is a nice gesture to invite the guests to come to your home to view the gifts, even if these guests are all included on the trousseau tea guest list. They will enjoy this more informal opportunity to "oh and ah" as they examine your treasures.

The Bachelor Dinner

I'm "agin" it! In my opinion, men do not enjoy getting together for a formal dinner "just for the boys." They enjoy fishing together, golfing together, or being spectators at sports activities together, but the only way they enjoy having dinner together is when dinner is on the way to or on the way back from Yankee Stadium, Table Rock Lake, or Tam O'Shanter Golf Course.

A bachelor dinner without benefit of other planned activity is nearly always reduced to a bacchanalian brawl. And there is no room in the kingdom of God for that kind of revelry.

If the groom wants to get the men in the wedding party together and has the time and money, he can plan an afternoon of golf or other recreation. But the formal dinner, just for men, is rapidly fading over the horizon—unless you happen to live in Washington, D. C., and your father is third undersecretary of agriculture.

The Out-of-Town Guests' Dinner

It is a happy idea to get together all the relatives and friends from out of town for lunch on the day of the wedding. The bride and her mother will be busy and do not have to go, but Aunt Minnie will enjoy assuming this hostess responsibility and the guests will feel that they are getting their money's worth out of their airline tickets. This is about the only opportunity they will have to hear something of how the romance began, and what the wedding will be like. If your dad isn't over in a corner of the den somewhere chewing his nails, he might be sent along as host to this group, especially if they are his people. This gives his people not only a chance to hear about the bride and groom, but to visit with one another. Most of them have not been together since Uncle Harry's funeral and that wasn't a very festive occasion.

Two dinners or lunches, or whatever, should be planned for the out-of-town guests. I heartily recommend a "to each his own" or the two-party system. Let the groom's Aunt Minnie entertain his relatives while your Aunt Minnie entertains your relatives. This is not the time for the "I'm so *happy* to meet you" overtures. (There'll be a profusion of this at the reception.) This is the time for kinfolk conversation like, "Is Bill really graduating from college this year?" and "Please do stay at our place while you attend the convention."

The Trousseau Tea

"Husband" and "trousseau" are two wedding words I especially like. The word "husband" is a derivative of an old Norwegian phrase *hous bonde*. A *hous bonde* is literally a peasant with a house. No matter how poor the Norwegian peasant might have been, his neighbors thought he should have a house of his own to bring his bride to, and they usually rallied around to help him build it. This brings us to another lesson in etymology. Trousseau is derived from the French word *trusse,* which means literally "a little bundle," and both the words came sliding down right out of Napoleon and Josephine's conversations into ours. And so does the custom of the bride's bringing her "trusse" or little bundle of worldly goods into her favorite peasant's house.

Today's groom, a long-time victor of the war on poverty, is not very peasantly, and today's bride has such a big "little bundle" for a trousseau that she spreads it throughout all the rooms in her mother's or grandmother's home, and invites all her friends, especially the givers of the wedding presents, to come and see. Sometimes the gifts are shown after the wedding as a part of the reception. But sometimes the bride and her mother give a trousseau tea and invite everyone to come, usually a few days before the wedding. The invitation can be handwritten or engraved, like this:

Mrs. Fred Wilson
Miss Marlene Wilson
Trousseau Tea
at their home
Tuesday, the second of June
from two to four o'clock

To display the gifts, you may rent folding tables, borrow them from your church, or even use sawhorses covered with plywood—they're all covered up anyway with lovely linen cloths.

Arrange your gifts in the loveliest way you can. Let the artist in you flourish. Group together linens, pretty sheets, towels, and table linens by colors.

Don't put exactly-the-sames together thereby embarrassing the three women who each gave you a set of pearl-handled steak knives. Arrange only one place setting of your china, silver, and crystal. At the side place a tiny card which will quietly convey the message that you have complete service for twelve.

You may display the gifts without the cards telling who gave them. But I think it is a nice compliment to the givers if you do. It will save you many an embarrassing moment of trying to remember who gave you the solid walnut salad bowl set and who gave you the teakwood one.

But you do not show off checks, money, or gift certificates. You may in good taste advise people you received these gifts by using little formal cards on which you write either "Check—$50," not listing the donor, or "Uncle Bill gave us a check for a barbecue grill."

Community custom, rather than any system of overall properness, seems to dictate whether or not you display your *personal* trousseau. I saw a trousseau last year, beautiful, all new, and tastefully laid out in the bride's own room, that made me wish I were going on my honeymoon all over again. Such lovely peignoirs and slippers! Such pretty shifts, bathing suits, and beach robes! Of course, the wedding gown and veil are never displayed. No one sees them, except your portrait photographer, until you walk down that aisle.

The receiving line at a trousseau tea is short—the mother of the bride and the bride. Sisters of the bride will probably be putting their talents to good use supervising the serving tables and assisting in the serving rooms. And here's another opportunity to be kind to your mother-in-law-to-be. You can bestow upon her the honor of being the first to pour the punch or tea. Then see that she has a reserved spot to sit—a *prominent* spot where she can greet all of the guests and chat with them. Refreshments can be as simple or elaborate as you want to make them.

I hope I've persuaded you to have a trousseau tea. It is one of the loveliest of all prenuptial parties and, in addition to giving you the pleasure of showing off your gifts, it gives the givers a certain amount of pleasure to know that you WANT to show them off. An invitation to a trousseau tea is another subtle way of saying thank you to all those people who are being so wonderful to you.

10

The Language of Flowers

How does your church feel about being decorated? The architect knew what he was doing when he designed your church sanctuary. Intense efforts have been poured forth by professional people (architects and interior decorators) and by people of spiritual concern (your church leadership) to make your sanctuary a place conducive to worship and communion with God. Do not try to redesign it into what you think might be a more suitable backdrop for your wedding. Use it as it is. Engage a floral decorator who will accept it *as it is* and whose decorations will enhance rather than detract from its loveliness.

Many church sanctuaries have been so abused through the years by well-meaning brides or florists that some churches have developed self-defense policies which must be followed by people responsible for wedding decorations. Here is a smattering of these policies which I've collected from several different churches representing many denominations:

The moving of church furniture is prohibited.
The obscuring of the baptistry or permanent decorations is forbidden.
Flowers must not be placed on the Lord's Supper table.
Simplicity of decorations is preferred over elaborate displays.
Do not obscure the organist's view of the processional and recessional aisles.

If candles are used, they must be properly shielded so that drippings do not reach the furniture or carpeting.

Heating, lighting, air-conditioning, and so on, are to be arranged for and operated only by some member of the church staff.

The sanctuary, dressing rooms, and reception rooms must be restored to the order in which they were found within a time limit after the ceremony. When a wedding is on Saturday, this time limit is, of necessity, quite short.

These are not the policies of any one church but, rather, selected portions of several policy statements which were held most in common by different churches. Be sure to check YOUR church's policy concerning decorations and give your florist a copy of it.

Choosing a Florist

There are three important factors to be considered in the selection of a florist. First, and most important, is his spiritual attitude— his "church manners." Once, with my own eyes, I watched a florist decorate a church altar for a wedding, all the while smoking a cigarette. When a member of the church staff suggested to him that it might be more appropriate not to smoke in the sanctuary, he stepped into the vestibule, threw the cigarette butt down on the floor, and ground it with the sole of his shoe into the tile. The custodian had already gone home, and that unattractive cigarette butt would have been there to greet the guests had it not been for the staff member who swooped it up in a Kleenex and discarded it—and, that might have set the church on fire.

So, when you are florist shopping, find one who can not only make an altar beautiful but who also has a beautiful attitude toward that altar. And the beautiful attitude he should have is *reverence*.

Second, you should select a florist who is reputed to do high quality work. When a florist knows how to make a wedding both personal and beautiful, the word soon gets around.

And third, if money matters to you (and I don't know very many people who enjoy complete immunity from mattering about money), make a list of your wedding requirements and get floral estimates. You do not need to do this if you are fortunate enough to live in a small town with a florist who has, over the years, established a good reputation. One of the ways he earned that good reputation was by being fair in money matters. But if you live in a big city you may save from fifty to seventy-five dollars by florist shopping. And you will soon discover that fifty or seventy-five dollars will buy a lot of ground beef.

Make a list of your floral needs as you think of them. Your florist will help you enlarge the list so that you will not leave out anything. Most florists use special order forms for this. Your list might include:

The bride's bouquet and going-away corsage

Maid of honor and bridesmaids' bouquets (how many?)

Corsages for two mothers, grandmothers, soloist, guest book attendant, reception assistants, and any others you may specify

Chancel Flowers

Candelabra

Prie-dieu (kneeling bench)

White aisle runner

Spotlight

Aisle ropes or ribbons

Pew markers

Street to door canopy

Portable central altar steps

Arrangements for reception and guest book table

Petals for flower girl

Boutonnieres for all the men in the wedding party, including the preacher, the grandfathers, and the ring bearer.

No doubt, you will want to have corsages for a few special people to wear at your wedding. Send a corsage to your married sister whom you would surely have chosen for your honor attendant had she not been pregnant. And what about your college housemother and the church hostess who have been so much help to you? Or maybe you'll want to remember with flowers that neighbor woman who made your wedding gown—even though you paid her to do it. Flowers are a special way to say thank you. There is something outstandingly beautiful about a bride who seems on her wedding day to be thinking of others rather than herself. (Actually she *did* the thinking weeks ago. She probably can't think at all on *the* day. But thoughtful gestures planned well in advance certainly convey the *feeling* that she is thinking about someone else, and that her thoughts are both kind and generous.)

Florists are extremely creative people. You may think of your bridesmaids' bouquets as being simply flowers. But when you say the phrase "bridesmaids' bouquets" to a florist, he immediately thinks:

> ring-shaped or basket-
> candle-wreathed or lover's knot
> parasol- or fan-shaped
> colonial nosegays or contemporary arrangements

And, if it happens to be the Christmas season, he might even think: snowball bouquets, muffs, or golden ornaments in pine branches. You will find that there is no limit to his imagination. And before long you will discover he has stimulated *your* imagination.

Flowers mirror your personality. Do some mental isometrics and picture in your mind:

> the daisy bride
> the orchid bride
> the magnolia bride
> the lily-of-the-valley bride

You see, there's a vast difference. All of these flowers are appropriate for weddings. But not all may be appropriate for *you*.

In addition to your personal preference, the season of the year will have a large bearing on the selection of your wedding flowers. For a springtime wedding you might want to use apple blossoms, cherry blossoms, forsythia, redbud, or dogwood to decorate the sanctuary. In the summer, roses, daisies, gladioli, and magnolias are plentiful. And in autumn, mums, asters, dahlias in amber and golden tones. In winter, roses and carnations add a lovely touch. I think the prettiest wedding I ever saw was a Christmas wedding. The altar was decorated with arrangements of bright red poinsettia, boughs of holly and pine, and the tall white tapers were set in gleaming brass, tree-style candelabra. The bridesmaids wore red velvet and the bride was absolutely radiant in white lace.

Besides personality and season, you may allow floral symbols to guide your selection. I do not know who thought up these symbols in the first place, and I doubt that the selection of daffodils for your bridesmaids' bouquet will insure joy in your marriage, but if you happen to be an incurable romanticist who likes to think on these things, here's food for thought:

Azalea	Devotion
Bleeding Heart	Fidelity
Camellia	Contentment
Carnation	Love (if red); Nuptials (if pink)
Cedar	Constancy
Cherry Blossoms	Chivalry
Chrysanthemum	Modesty
Daffodil	Joy
Daisy	Innocence, Youth, Simplicity
Forget-Me-Not	Faith and Hope
Gardenia	Purity
Holly	Protection
Hyacinth	Constancy
Ivy	Immortality
Lily	Innocence, Purity
Magnolia	Virtue
Pine	Strength, Loyalty
Rose	Love, Beauty

If perchance you have persuaded your father to read this chapter, or to look over your flower list, the only symbol he is aware of is the dollar sign. It will be some consolation for him to learn that, though all the flowers are generally ordered by the bride on one list, the groom pays for the bridal bouquet; a corsage for the bride's going-away ensemble (sometimes lifted from the center of the bouquet); corsages for the bride's mother, his mother, grand-mothers, and other honored guests; boutonnieres for himself, the minister, the best man, the groomsmen or ushers, his father, male soloist, and organist. The florist will send separate statements.

You may save some money on your decorations by checking with your church secretary to see what wedding equipment your church owns. Our church, for example, makes available to our brides two sets of candelabra, portable central altar steps, and many reception accessories, including ceiling to floor draperies which, on these special occasions, completely shut off the kitchen from the reception hall.

Also, if economy is your watchword, go lightly on the flowers and heavy on feathery foliage and candles. I am a candle lover and delight in the quiet glow of an evening candlelight wedding. Plan to set tall white tapers in several candelabra. Use candles on the window sills, at the guest book table, and on the reception tables. The candlelight is sometimes augmented by a spotlight directed on the prie-dieu.

Fire laws in some cities prohibit the use of many candles, which I suppose is wise, but it is very unromantic. If such is your situation, you may be able to use hurricane lamps—candles enclosed in lamp globes, which might set the theme for an Early American wedding. Or, you could use battery-powered candles, which are rather expensive but worth the investment, I think. They may be ordered from the Gamble Hinged Music Company, in Chicago, Illinois.

There are some over-and-above florists who happily provide for you: etiquette books; picture books of wedding floral arrangements; names of caterers, photographers; spotlight; long, long tablecloths for reception tables; ring bearer's pillow; flower girl's basket.

If you plan to dress at church, some florists even provide a mirror, coverings for the floor to keep your white gown white, and a special "emergency kit" which contains, among other things, smelling salts, sandpaper to rough the soles of your new shoes, white chalk to quickly cover a smudge on a white dress when it is too late to do anything else about it, and Alka-Seltzer.

The over-and-above florist I know adds a sentimental touch. She attaches two miniature bluebirds to the *back* of the bride's bouquet, just above the handle, where the bride can see them as she looks down at her bouquet. These are the bluebirds of happiness, she explains, and are the something "blue" for your wedding. They also are part of her wishes for your future happiness.

Now who would object to paying a bill to a florist like that?

11

Pictures for Tomorrow

This lovely time of life for you is being engraved bit by bit somewhere in a corner of your mind, and will live forever there as a collection of memories. Even so, you will want to make a visual record of your wedding, so that you can share these pretty memories with special people yet to come into your life—like your children.

A beautifully bound white leather book, filled with photographs, is the conventional, tangible way to preserve your wedding for posterity. So it is important that the pictures in the book be exactly the same as your pretty memories.

Be very choosy when selecting the *one* photographer from among all the available photographers listed in your yellow pages. Go photographer shopping. If you are too timid to venture into their studios and ask to see samples of their wedding work, then, by all means, look at the wedding albums of your friends and when you discover sets of pictures you like, ask who made them.

Once you discover a photographer whose work pleases you, go to his studio and talk with him. See samples of his work and learn the cost. Find out if he will respect and work within YOUR time schedule, so that you won't have to adjust your life on your busiest day to fit into HIS time schedule.

One of the most important things you will want to ask is whether or not he makes available light photographs made quietly from the back of the sanctuary during the wedding ceremony. Many churches understandably forbid the distraction of flash bulbs during the wedding ceremony. Do not be disappointed if you find this to be true in your church. Available light pictures are much better than flash pictures anyway. With the use of candlelight (sometimes helped out by a spotlight from the balcony), the scenes of your wedding ceremony evolve from your good photographer's light meter into your memory book, capturing the exact beauty of the wedding—your white dress shimmering against a soft backdrop of darkness, broken here and there by other whites: the white dinner jackets, the white aisle cloth and soft shadows, and punctuated by the bright candle flames. Available light photographs have an ethereal quality about them that brightly lighted wedding pictures do not have. I like them much better than flash pictures.

If you can find a photographer who uses this medium you can preserve moments of your wedding in the sanctuary that otherwise would be forever lost—you and the groom in prayer at the altar, surrounded by your attendants, and that special moment, the wedding kiss, which can never *really* be reenacted after the ceremony just for a photographer's benefit. So, remember that important phrase, *available light.* Find a photographer who uses it and ask to see samples of his work.

Keep to a bare minimum the formal, posed pictures that must be made in the sanctuary after the guests have gone—and before the reception can begin. You may want to redo the giving and receiving of the ring, you may want a bride-and-groom-look-at-each-other type picture, and, maybe one showing the wedding party at the altar.

I do not recommend calling together the whole wedding party, complete with ushers and grandmothers, to pose for a formal picture. In the first place, it takes too much time and in the second place, what have you got when it's finished? Just a group of faces, all very small because the group is large.

It is much better to have several candid shots. Advise the photographer to be sure to catch everyone of the wedding party at one time or another.

Some of the usual candids are: (1) The bride's mother and maid of honor adjusting her veil; (2) the bride showing her pretty garter to a wondering flower girl while the bridesmaids look on; (3) the pastor, seated at his desk, giving last-minute instructions to the groom and his best man; (4) the guest book attendant handing a pen to a guest; (5) the ushers rolling out the aisle cloth; (6) one usher about to seat the groom's mother, with groom's father following; (7) the bridesmaids' examining their pretty bouquets; (8) the ring bearer in conversation with the flower girl; (9) the bride on her father's arm, ready to enter the sanctuary; (10) the bride and groom as they lead the recessional out of the sanctuary; (11) the reception line at the very beginning, so it will not be backs or sides of people; (12) the bride and groom cutting the cake; (13) the reception assistants—functioning; (14) the bride throwing her bouquet; (15) the bride and groom leaving the church; (16) the newlyweds in the getaway car, usually bearing all manner of decorations.

Ask your photographer to make a "posed candid" of the soloist and organist *before* the wedding. They are always among the first at the church anyway.

In this manner you can have a picture of everyone—your attendants, your families, your assistants—without having to pose for an hour with first one and then the other. Granted, some of these listed are not really "candid" in the full sense of the word, but they *look* candid once they are made and put away in your book.

Make a list of candids you want and leave it in the hands of your photographer. Do not have the customary pictures unless you want them. If you don't want to go through that awkward ceremony of feeding the groom a sticky piece of cake and likewise choking one down when it's his turn to feed you, TELL your photographer in advance. Say instead that you want simply a picture of the two of you, his hand guiding yours, as you cut the first slice of cake.

Remember to have someone ready to take snapshots at all of your prenuptial parties. And have someone primed to take a few color snapshots before and after your wedding. Black and white doesn't do justice to the bridesmaids' dresses and bouquets. On the other hand, don't have all of your pictures made in color. Space-age science is pretty wonderful, but it hasn't yet convinced me that these colors will never fade. Even if they fool me and don't fade, they are difficult to preserve because they tend to stick to any surface placed against them—like the opposite page in your wedding scrapbook.

Your Wedding Portrait

You will want to have your wedding portrait made in your photographer's studio as soon as your wedding dress and veil are ready. This finished picture can then be sent to the newspaper society editor, along with the vital statistics of your wedding. It should be marked with a release date very soon after your wedding.

Your society editor will be your mother's important guide here, just as she was in the announcement of your engagement. Some papers want the whole scoop—who did what and who wore what. Others want only a bare minimum of facts. The society page I read most often lists the bride's maiden name; the groom's name; date and time of wedding; place of wedding; and officiating minister. Then it gives a detailed description of the decorations used; names of the organist and soloist; what the soloist sang; and exactly how the bride looked.

"Given in marriage by her father, the bride wore a floor-length gown, styled with silk organza skirt and Chantilly lace bodice. Motifs of similar lace were appliquéd near the hem of the skirt and outlined the chapel train. The bride's elbow-length veil of silk illusion and lace was attached to a pearl crown. She carried a colonial bouquet of white gardenias, pink sweetheart roses and stephanotis, with streamers tied in sweetheart knots."

The maid of honor gets full treatment in our paper, too.

"Miss Sarah Belshe attended her sister as maid of honor, attired in pale blue chiffon over taffeta. The floor-length gown, styled on Empire lines, had a bodice overlaid with lace, designed with a scoop neckline and long sleeves. A small bow accented the back of the waistline. Miss Belshe wore matching shoes and a small veil headpiece centered with a tulle rosette. She carried a nosegay of blue asters, lavender stephanotis and baby's breath, tied with blue streamers."

The bridesmaids, too, are listed and descriptions of their dresses and flowers are given in minute detail.

The best man and ushers are named.

The costumes of the mothers are described.

Reception information is given in detail.

"Following the ceremony a reception was held at the home of the bride's parents. A four-tiered, all-white wedding cake was centered on a table covered with a Venise lace cloth over blue. White gardenias and small blue and lavender flowers and smilax encircled the cake and extended down the table, connecting two triple-branched silver candelabra with aerial arrangements of blue and lavender flowers with smilax. Matching silver compotes were filled with nuts and mints.

"The circular punch table, covered in lace, held a crystal bowl filled with blue punch in which floated blue and lavender flowers frozen in an ice ring. White gardenias and small lavender and blue flowers were combined with smilax to garland the punch bowl."

Reception assistants are listed.

Details of the bride's going-away costume are given.

The couple's new home address is given.

Out-of-town guests are frequently listed.

Don't worry, you don't have to think up all these lovely phrases. Your florist will furnish the phrases he chooses to describe his work, and the shop where you purchased your gown and the bridesmaids' gowns will furnish glowing descriptions.

There are a few other ways of preserving your wedding memories. One important way is the use of a tape recorder. The microphone can be hidden among the ivy to record your "I do's" for you to hear forever after.

And if your brother is a home-movie addict, he can capture the madness of the preparation on the wedding morning—the leaving for the church, the festivities of your reception—and you can relive all these joyous events on long winter evenings by your hearthside.

I hope you have better luck preserving your wedding for posterity than we did! While my engagement picture and notice were waiting in the society editor's office to be released, the newspaper plant burned down! And it was not rebuilt until after our wedding. As if that weren't enough, I chose a wedding memoir book with a taffeta-like, padded cover. During the Kansas floods of 1951, we lived in a damp basement apartment in Lawrence, and the book and most of the pictures were ruined by mildew!

I'm not sure what the moral of my sad story is, but I've been wanting to complain about it for years—and this seemed such an appropriate place!

12

The Rehearsal

The wedding rehearsal, ordinarily held the evening before the wedding, can be a pleasure or a pain. It is more likely to be pleasurable than painful if the planning of the rehearsal is already accomplished in a quiet premarital counseling session in the pastor's study weeks, or at least days, before. Your pastor will help you decide on an order of service. The simple order would include:

Organ prelude
Entrance of the minister, groom, and best man
Entrance of the bridesmaids and maid of honor
Entrance of the bride on right arm of her father
Ceremony
Recessional
Receiving line in foyer
A more elaborate wedding would call for the:
Organ prelude
Lighting of the candles
Seating of the groom's mother
Seating of the bride's mother
Drawing of the ribbons to seal the aisle
Drawing of the white aisle cloth
Special music—vocal or instrumental
Entrance of the minister, groom, best man, groomsmen

Entrance of the bridesmaids
Entrance of the maid of honor
Entrance of the ring bearer
Entrance of the flower girl
Entrance of the bride on arm of her father
Ceremony (may include spoken vows and musical prayers)
The kiss (if your church policies allow)
Recessional
Ushering out of mothers, families, and honored guests
Ushering out of all guests, row by row, front to back of church.

You will want to decide on your order of service well in advance of your rehearsal, have it approved by your minister, and then leave it in his hands.

All etiquette authorities, barring none, say that the minister is the final authority on the ceremony and that his rehearsal instructions must be followed without question. Yet, *nobody* seems to read this advice any more. As a result, we have an abundance of rehearsal directors: aunts, mothers, brides, professional wedding managers, and even—perish the thought!—minister's wives. Let the *minister* do it. Tell him all your wishes in advance and he will carry them out. He is trained to do this. Even if he weren't, he undoubtedly has more wedding experience than anyone else present at the rehearsal.

Most ministers feel very strongly about this because they have seen the havoc that results from having too many rehearsal directors. One of our minister friends sums up the feelings of a good many ministers when he says:

I do not care what authorities the bride and groom consult, where they go for help, or even how strange their ideas may be. But I do expect them to go over these ideas with me sometime well in advance of the wedding. Then, when rehearsal time comes, I, *as minister*, am in charge. I do not demand this because I want to be the "big man," but rather for two positive reasons:

First, a wedding is a religious service. That the bride and groom understand this is evidenced by their choosing a house of God for the place of their wedding and a minister of Christ to officiate. Therefore, I am most reluctant to turn a divine service over to a theatrical director.

Second, I cannot abide a disorganized rehearsal. As you well know, if the bride's mother, the bride, the professional consultant, the groom's mother, and the minister each tries to conduct the rehearsal, confusion reigns.

Therefore, I tell both the bride and the groom that they are not obligated to have me as their minister. But if they do choose me, they must accept my judgment once we have arrived at a ceremony that seems to please them.

So, that's who is in charge, and you'll find that he runs a pretty neat ship.

Now, who comes to the rehearsal? All who take part in the wedding must come.

The bride and groom

Maid of honor and best man

Groomsmen, ushers, and bridesmaids

Parents of both bride and groom

The musicians

Flower girl

Ring bearer

Pages

Candlelighters, if other than ushers.

Though they do not participate, the parents or husbands and wives of members of the wedding party may attend. Personally, I enjoy attending the rehearsal dinner, but not the rehearsal. I prefer to attend the wedding as any other guest and attending the rehearsal takes a little of the joy away from watching the actual wedding.

There is an old and ridiculous superstition that the bride should not participate in her own rehearsal but should use a stand-in. She'll have bad luck if she rehearses, we are warned. Nonsense! She is far more likely to have bad luck if she doesn't practice her part in the wedding. Everything will go much more smoothly if the bride is filled with poise and confidence that comes from the awareness of what to do next. And we are trying to abide by Christian principles, not superstitions!

Parts to Be Rehearsed

Lighting of the candles.—Preferably, this rehearsing should be done with the same musical background that will be used during the actual wedding service, because it establishes the tempo for the candlelighters. Candlelighters should practice lighting slowly, gracefully, and staying together. They should check each other with corner-of-the-eye glances rather than constant head turning. They should agree in advance to wait on each other. If one candle is stubborn and virtually refuses to ignite, the other candlelighter should wait. In this way, they will finish at the same time. They should light the candles in the same order from the lowest to the highest, and when they have finished they turn, each toward the outside of the church, and assume their predesignated places, either reserved pews or places in the wedding party.

The drawing of the ribbons.—If ribbons are used to seal the aisle, two ushers will advance to the front of the church, about the fourth or fifth pew back—wherever the reserved section for the families and special guests ends, and pick up the streamers which the florist has affixed to the end of the pew. They will walk together then, in nice even strides, laying the streamers over the backs of all the pews next to the aisle, and finally securing the ribbons with the loop the florist has provided to the very back pew. This is usually done when a church has only one central aisle, but it can be done if a church has more than one aisle. It just takes more ushers—two to each aisle.

The drawing of the aisle cloth.—The white aisle canvas on which the bride will walk to the altar is secured either in accordian fashion or on some type of a roller at the altar. Two ushers will, at the appropriate time, advance to the altar, each take a corner of the aisle canvas, and together unroll it to the back of the church. Sometimes this is done as soon as the bride's mother is seated and the ribbons drawn. At other weddings, it is done just before the flower girl and the bride make their entrances. Whenever it is done, it is a lovely part of the wedding service and can add much to the occasion.

Seating of the groom's mother.—She is escorted to her seat by an usher who offers her his right arm. If a groom's brother is serving as usher, he should certainly have the honor of seating his mother. The groom's father, brothers, and sisters are already seated in the family pew. Or the father may walk behind the usher and the mother. In any case, the mother should be given the aisle seat, second pew, right side of the church. She is the most honored guest at the wedding.

Seating of the bride's mother.—The bride's mother is the last person to be seated. She is the hostess. After she has been seated no other guests are allowed to enter. The ushers can be instructed to guide them quietly to the balcony or to slip them in a wing, but never under any circumstances should they enter the main sanctuary after the bride's mother has been seated. She, too, takes the usher's right arm, even though she will step to the left to be seated. The usher can, after she has relinquished his arm, turn smoothly and see that she is seated before making the trip back up the aisle.

The processional.—The minister, the groom, and best man enter from the vestry. Sometimes the other men in the wedding party come from the front of the church—from the vestry or minister's office. But sometimes they march in from the back of the church with the entire wedding party. They can either walk in front of the bridesmaids or two by two with the bridesmaids, or one with each bridesmaid. At the altar they may stand to the right with the best man, or you may wish to have a mixture of bridesmaids and groomsmen in juxtaposition on both sides of the altar. This is just one of the many decisions you should make well in advance and advise your minister. Then he will direct the processional as you have planned it.

It is best that the processional be rehearsed to its musical accompaniment. But, if you have a wedding consultant, mother, aunt, or other perfectionist type female who insists that the women of the wedding party practice methods of walking down the aisle, I suggest that this be done at another time so that you and the girls will not take up the time of all the other people involved in the rehearsal.

The half-step or skating step is out of vogue. All that is really necessary is that the bridesmaids walk gracefully and in a reasonable tempo to the music, and that members of the wedding party space themselves eight paces, or four or five pews apart. I have watched people practice *the way to walk* for hours on end and could really tell no difference at all in the way they walked at their weddings than in the way totally unpracticed people walked. It's all a matter of graceful carriage, and if you don't have it by the eve of your wedding, you are not going to develop it in a few hours—even with practice.

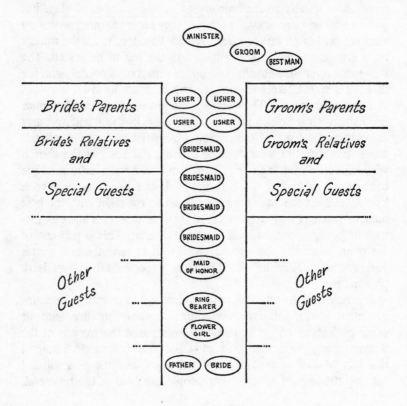

The recessional.—At the cue from the minister, the organist will start the lovely strains of the "Wedding March" and you will take the groom's right arm. Your maid of honor will carefully adjust your train, so that it will turn around conveniently when you do. She then will hand your bouquet to you and you and the groom will lead the recessional back down the center aisle, or, in a two aisle church, down the right aisle toward the back of the church. The recessional music has a lively tempo, but don't let it stir you into walking too fast. All those people in all those pews want a glimpse of your lovely gown and a look at your smiling face.

The children in the wedding party follow next, with a little urging from the bridesmaid in charge of them. Then the maid of honor and best man fall in, followed by the ushers and bridesmaids two by two. As a rule, the minister stands in his place until the wedding party has reached the back of the church and is out of the sanctuary. He then exits to his office or vestry.

The ceremony.—The actual reading or reciting of the ceremony is not done at the rehearsal. But your minister will ask you to rehearse the giving and receiving of the rings, perhaps the kneeling, and sometimes any speaking parts you have in the ceremony.

Musicians.—The soloists usually attend the rehearsal to learn their cues. They may sing a few bars, but they need not rehearse the whole number. They do their actual rehearsing and polishing at another time. Remember, no one should take up time rehearsing some portion of the wedding which could be rehearsed just as well after everyone else has gone.

Length of rehearsal.—The rehearsal should never last more than an hour, even for the most formal wedding. The rehashing of minute details is inclined to have an adverse, rather than a good, effect on the final outcome. It only tends to make the wedding party nervous and tired.

Your pastor will probably close your wedding rehearsal with prayer, asking God's blessing on your wedding. (You might tell him you would like for him to do this.) This direct communication with God will impress upon the members of your wedding party the spiritual importance of your wedding. And, in retrospect, the rehearsal will seem much smoother when it ends with these quiet moments of reverence.

The Rehearsal Dinner

One way to insure that the rehearsal will be short is to arrange to have the dinner afterward, rather than before, though either is proper. You may plan the rehearsal for five-thirty and the dinner for seven, or the dinner for six and the rehearsal following—or whatever combination is most convenient to you and the members of your wedding party.

The rehearsal dinner may be given by either set of parents. It is usually given by the groom's parents unless they live some distance away or for some other reason cannot assume the responsibility. Even some who do live far away arrange to give the rehearsal dinner, making all plans by correspondence with a hotel, club, or restaurant.

The dinner is customarily a rather formal affair with the tables lavishly decorated with floral centerpieces and wedding motifs. It is nice to plan a tasteful menu, but do not bother to provide a gourmet's repast. Don't waste your lobster Newburg on this aggregation. They are by this time so numbed by a combination of exhaustion and excitement that everything will taste pretty much the same. Food is food and fellowship is fellowship. *Tomorrow* is the important day, not *tonight*.

The rehearsal dinner is the best time for the bride and groom to give the attendants their gifts. Excitement is mounting and everyone is in a gay and appreciative mood. These gifts are to be selected by you as thank you's to all your attendants and musicians (unless they are impersonally hired). The groom provides gifts also for the men of the wedding party.

Your jeweler will happily suggest any number of gifts for both women and men in the wedding party. They may be identical, or you may want to select individual surprises, as you would Christmas gifts, with the personality of the receiver in mind.

Whatever the selection, the gifts should be beautifully wrapped and distributed at the rehearsal dinner with a "This-is-to-say-thank-you!" flourish.

If neither your parents nor the groom's parents can afford a full course rehearsal dinner, it is perfectly acceptable to have a dessert party after the rehearsal and distribute the gifts then. This still provides the backdrop necessary for members of the wedding party to socialize and to get better acquainted.

One important thing to remember on your wedding eve is "early to bed" makes a beautiful bride. Neither rehearsal, nor dinner, nor party should go on ad infinitum!

13

Your Shining Moment

The church is lovelier than you've ever seen it. The flowers, the candlelight, the music—all seem even more wonderful than you had planned. At the altar the minister, the groom, and the wedding party are waiting. The white aisle cloth glistens. A flower girl drops dainty rose petals in your pathway. Then suddenly the music swells into a crescendo. You clutch the arm of your father a little tighter, but you remember to smile. This is your shining moment. The congregation stands and all eyes focus upon you as you walk toward the altar.

"We are now about to hear the wedding vows of," the minister begins, and you are lost in the wonder and the holiness of it all. This is as it should be, for it is one of the highest spiritual moments of your life, a time for commitment to God and to your husband.

Just in case you will be too enraptured with it all to hear the ceremony then, please study it now. Your pastor will want to go over HIS ceremony with you before your wedding, and most ministers are willing to make minor adjustments to please you. There is no such thing as a "standard" Protestant ceremony, referred to in most books of wedding etiquette. Ministers are at liberty to choose their own phrases which will make up the ceremony in which you and your groom will declare your love for each other and pledge your faith to each other.

There are three basic types of Christian wedding ceremonies: the individual personal ceremony based on Bible truths, the ceremony phrased almost entirely in biblical language, and the traditional form for the solemnization of matrimony, sometimes called the Episcopal service.

I am including three ceremonies in this book—not for your use but for your study, so that you will know generally and specifically what a marriage ceremony says.

The ceremony I like best was my father's. He used it on that Sunday afternoon in June, years ago, at my wedding. My husband, also a minister, uses it now with slight variations, and every time I hear him recite it, I can still hear my father's tender voice and see in my mind's eye the smiling young groom that met me at the altar.

Daddy's Ceremony

At the hour of the marriage, when the party is assembled at the altar, the minister shall say:

Dearly beloved, we are now about to hear the wedding vows of Miss ——————— and Mr. ———————. May I ask who presents the bride?

Then shall the father of the bride answer,

I do. (Or, Her mother and I do.)

Then shall the minister say to the father:

Thank you, Mr. ———————. You are to be commended for bringing such a charming daughter (or lovely daughter or sweet daughter, as the case may be) to the altar.

The father of the bride, having given her in marriage, shall take his seat by the bride's mother, and the minister shall continue:

May our Heavenly Father look down upon us with his smile of approval. May the Lord Jesus Christ be present and add his blessing. May the Holy Spirit attend and seal these vows in love. For marriage is a divine ordinance given to promote social order and to increase human happiness. When God created man he saw that it was not good for him to live alone, and so prepared for him a helpmeet. He took not the woman from his head, lest she should rule over him, nor from his feet, lest he should trample upon her, but from his side, that she should be equal with him, and from close to his heart, that he should love, cherish, and protect her.

Marriage was honored by the presence of Christ at the marriage feast in Cana of Galilee and used by him as an emblem of that great day when he, the bridegroom, adorned in all his glory, shall come for the church which he has purchased with his own blood, and who shall be dressed in the spotless garment of his righteousness.

Marriage was commended by the apostle Paul, speaking through the Holy Spirit, as being honorable in all things. A marriage made in heaven is a union of two lives—two hearts that beat as one—so welded together that they walk together; they work and labor together. They bear each other's burdens, they share each other's joys. I want to remind you that you are to cultivate the habit of living together, that you are to be congenial, loving, and tenderhearted, forbearing one another in love, and remembering that the vows which you are now about to take are as binding in adversity as they are in prosperity, that these vows are to be broken only by death.

Then shall the minister direct the couple:

I will ask you now to unite right hands.

> *The bride hands her bouquet and Bible to her maid of honor at this point and places her right hand in the right hand of the groom.*
>
> *Then shall the minister ask the groom:*

Will you ——————— take ——————— as your wedded wife, to live together after God's ordinance in the holy estate of matrimony?

Will you promise to love her, comfort her, honour and keep her, and forsaking all others cleave only to her, so long as you both shall live?

> *Then the groom shall reply:*

I will.

> *Then shall the minister ask the bride:*

Will you ——————— take ——————— as your wedded husband, to live together after God's ordinance in the holy estate of matrimony? Do you promise to love him, obey him, honour and keep him, and forsaking all others cleave only to him, until death do you part?

> *Then the bride shall reply:*

I will.

> *Then shall the minister ask the couple together:*

Do you solemnly promise before Almighty God and in the presence of these witnesses to receive each other as husband and wife, pledging yourselves to love each other, and to make every reasonable exertion to promote each other's happiness until the union into which you are now entering is dissolved by death.

> *Then shall the bride and groom each declare:*

I do.

> *The minister shall continue:*

I will ask you then to seal the vows which you have just made by the giving and receiving of these rings. The circle is the emblem of eternity and gold is the symbol of all that is pure and holy, and our prayer is that your love and your happiness will be as unending as the rings. These rings are a remembrance and in the years to come they will remind you of this happy hour, and my prayer is that you will be as happy then as you are now.

> *Then shall the minister direct the groom*
> *to place the ring upon the bride's finger*
> *and to repeat after him, phrase at a time:*

With this ring I thee wed. I take thee —————, to have and to hold, to love and to cherish, in sickness and in health, for richer for poorer, for better for worse, until death do us part.

> *Then shall the minister direct the bride to*
> *place the ring upon the groom's finger and*
> *to repeat after him, phrase at a time:*

With this ring I thee wed. I take thee —————, to have and to hold, to love and to cherish, in sickness and in health, for richer for poorer, for better for worse, so long as we both shall live.

> *Then shall the couple declare in unison*
> *together:*

"Whither thou goest, I will go; and where thou lodgest, I will lodge: thy people shall be my people, and thy God my God." *

> *Then shall the minister pronounce:*

And now, according to the laws of this great country in which we live, and by my authority as a minister of the gospel, I pronounce you husband and wife, and what God has joined together, let not man put asunder.

> *Then shall the minister lead in prayer.*

The Biblical Language Ceremony

A very good friend of ours uses a ceremony full of quotations taken directly from the Bible. He used this first at his sister's wed-

---

* Take note. This beautiful promise was first made, not to a husband, but to a mother-in-law (cf. Ruth 1:16)!

ding, and the couple being married helped select the Scriptures in advance. This, too, is a beautiful ceremony:

> *At the hour of the marriage, when the*
> *party is assembled at the altar the minister*
> *shall say:*

We are gathered together in the sight of God, and in the face of this company, to join together this man and this woman in holy matrimony. Marriage is the first institution given for the welfare of the human race. In the ancient bowers of Eden, before the tempter had touched the world, God saw that it was not good for the man to be alone. He made a helpmeet suitable for him and established the rite of marriage, while heavenly hosts witnessed the wonderful scene.

Originated in divine wisdom and goodness, designed to promote human happiness and holiness, this rite is the foundation of home life and social order, and so must remain till the end of time. It was sanctioned and honored by the presence and power of Jesus at the marriage in Cana of Galilee, and marked the beginning of his wondrous works. It was commended of Paul to be honorable among all men. It is the most important step in life and, therefore, is not to be entered into unadvisedly or lightly, but reverently, discreetly, advisedly, and in the fear of God. Who giveth this woman in marriage?

> *Then shall the father of the bride answer:*

I do. (Or, Her mother and I do.)

> *The father of the bride, having given his*
> *daughter in marriage shall take his seat by*
> *the bride's mother, and the minister shall*
> *continue:*

From God's Holy Book we read these words: From the beginning of the creation God made them male and female. And the Lord God said, It is not good that the man should be alone; I will make a helpmeet for him. For this cause shall a man leave his father and mother, and cleave to his wife; And they twain shall be one flesh: so then

they are no more twain, but one flesh. Wives, submit yourselves
unto your own husbands, as unto the Lord. For the husband is the
head of the wife, even as Christ is the head of the church: and he is
the Saviour of the body.

Therefore as the church is subject unto Christ, so let the wives be
to their own husbands in every thing.

Husbands, love your wives, even as Christ also loved the church,
and gave himself for it.

So ought men to love their wives as their own bodies. He that
loveth his wife loveth himself.

Nevertheless let every one of you in particular so love his wife
even as himself; and the wife see that she reverence her husband.

You, ——————, and you, ——————, have come to me signifying your desire to be formally united in marriage, and being
assured that no legal, moral, or religious barriers hinder this proper
union, I command you to join your right hands and give heed to the
questions now asked you.

*Then shall the minister direct the follow-
ing specifically to the groom:*

——————, in taking the woman whom you hold by the right
hand to be your lawful and wedded wife, I require you to promise
to love and cherish her, to honor and sustain her, in sickness and in
health, in poverty as in wealth, in the bad that may darken your
days, in the good that may lighten your ways, and to be true to her
in all things until death alone shall part you.

Do you so promise?

Then shall the groom promise:

I do.

*And the minister shall direct the following
specifically to the bride:*

——————, in taking the man who holds you by the right hand
to be your lawful and wedded husband, I require you to promise to

love and cherish him, to honor and sustain him, in sickness as in health, in poverty as in wealth, in the bad that may darken your days, in the good that may lighten your ways, and to be true to him in all things until death alone shall part you.

Do you so promise?

Then shall the bride promise:

I do.

The minister then continues:

A new commandment I give unto you, That ye love one another; as I have loved you, that ye also love one another.

Love suffereth long, and is kind; love envieth not; love vaunteth not itself, is not puffed up.

Doth not behave itself unseemly, seeketh not her own, is not easily provoked, thinketh no evil; rejoiceth not in iniquity, but rejoiceth in the truth.

Beareth all things, believeth all things, hopeth all things, endureth all things.

Love never faileth, for love is of God.

And now abideth faith, hope, love, these three; but the greatest of these is love.

*Then shall the minister take in his hand
the ring for the bride and continue:*

The ring is a symbol of the love you have for each other. Its unending circle represents the eternal quality of your love and the gold represents the purity of that love. As a ceaseless reminder of this hour and as a seal of the vows you take, you will now give and receive your rings.

To the groom he will say:

Do you —————— give this ring to —————— as a token of your love for her?

The groom shall answer:

I do.

*The minister shall then direct the groom
to repeat after him:*

I, —————, take thee, —————, to be my wedded wife,
to have and to hold from this day forward, for better for worse, for
richer for poorer, in sickness and in health, to love and to cherish,
till death do us part, according to God's holy ordinance, and thereto
I pledge thee my love.

Then shall the minister ask the bride:

Will you, —————, take this ring as a token of —————'s
love for you, and will you wear it as a token of your love for him?

Then shall the bride promise:

I will.

Then the minister will say to the bride:

Do you, —————, give this ring to ————— as a token
of your love for him?

And the bride shall promise:

I do.

*The minister shall then direct the bride to
repeat after him:*

I, —————, take thee, —————, to be my wedded hus-
band, to have and to hold, from this day forward, for better for
worse, for richer for poorer, in sickness and in health, to love and
to cherish, till death do us part, according to God's holy ordinance,
and thereto I pledge thee my love.

The minister shall then ask the groom:

Will you, —————, take this ring as a token of —————'s
love for you, and will you wear it as a token of your love for her?

The groom shall then promise:

I will.

The minister shall then lead in prayer.
(Sometimes a wedding prayer is sung.)
Then the minister continues:

Thou shalt love the Lord thy God with all thine heart, and with all thy soul, and with all thy might.

And these words, which I command thee this day, shall be in thine heart: And thou shalt teach them diligently unto thy children, and shalt talk of them when thou sittest in thine house.

Put on therefore, as the elect of God, kindness, humbleness of mind, meekness, longsuffering;

Forbearing one another, and forgiving one another.

And above all these things put on love, which is the bond of perfectness.

And let the peace of God rule in your hearts.

Having pledged your faith in, and love to each other, and having sealed your solemn marital vows by giving and receiving the rings, acting in the authority vested in me by the laws of this state, and looking to heaven for divine sanction, I pronounce you husband and wife in the presence of God and these assembled witnesses.

What therefore God hath joined together, let not man put asunder.

And now may the God of peace prosper and bless you in this new relationship, and may the grace of Jesus Christ abound unto you now and forevermore.

The Ceremony of Solemnization of Matrimony

Most ceremonies are based on a very old ceremony called the Episcopal Marriage Service Ceremony. Many Protestant ministers, other than the Episcopal clergymen, use this ceremony in its original form, and still many others use variations of it. Here it is for your study:

At the day and time appointed for solem-
nization of matrimony, the persons to be
married shall come into the body of the
church, or shall be ready in some proper
house, with their friends and neighbors;
and there standing together, the man on
the right hand, and the woman on the left,
the minister shall say:

Dearly beloved, we are gathered together here in the sight of God, and in the face of this company, to join together this man and this woman in holy matrimony, which is an honourable estate, instituted of God, signifying unto us the mystical union that is betwixt Christ and his church: which holy estate Christ adorned and beautified with his presence and first miracle that he wrought in Cana of Galilee, and is commended of Saint Paul to be honourable among all men: and therefore is not by any to be entered into unadvisedly or lightly; but reverently, discreetly, advisedly, soberly, and in the fear of God. Into this holy estate these two persons present come now to be joined. If any man can show just cause, why they may not lawfully be joined together, let him now speak, or else hereafter forever hold his peace.

And also speaking unto the persons who
are to be married, he shall say:

I REQUIRE and charge you both, as ye will answer at the dreadful day of judgment when the secrets of all hearts shall be disclosed, that if either of you know any impediment, why ye may not be lawfully joined together in matrimony, ye do now confess it. For be ye well assured, that if any persons are joined together otherwise than as God's Word doth allow, their marriage is not lawful.

The minister, if he shall have reason to
doubt of the lawfulness of the proposed
marriage, may demand sufficient surety
for his indemnification; but if no impedi-

*ment shall be alleged, or suspected, the
minister shall say to the man:*

——————, wilt thou have this woman to thy wedded wife, to
live together after God's ordinance in the holy estate of matrimony?
Wilt thou love her, comfort her, honour, and keep her in sickness
and in health; and, forsaking all others, keep thee only unto her, so
long as ye both shall live?

The man shall answer:

I will.

*Then shall the minister say unto the
woman:*

——————, wilt thou have this man to thy wedded husband,
to live together after God's ordinance in the holy estate of matrimony? Wilt thou love him, comfort him, honour, and keep him in
sickness and in health; and, forsaking all others, keep thee only
unto him, so long as ye both shall live?

The woman shall answer:

I will.

Then the minister shall say,

Who giveth this woman to be married to this man?

*Then shall they give their troth to each
other in this manner. The minister, receiving the woman at her father's or
friend's hands, shall cause the man with
his right hand to take the woman by her
right hand, and to say after him as fol-
loweth:*

I, ——————, take thee, ——————, to my wedded wife, to
have and to hold from this day forward, for better for worse, for
richer for poorer, in sickness and in health, to love and to cherish,

till death us do part, according to God's holy ordinance; and thereto I plight thee my troth.

> *Then shall they loose their hands; and the woman with her right hand taking the man by his right hand, shall likewise say after the minister,*

I, —————, take thee, —————, to my wedded husband, to have and to hold from this day forward, for better for worse, for richer for poorer, in sickness and in health, to love and to cherish, till death us do part, according to God's holy ordinance; and thereto I give thee my troth.

> *Then shall they again loose their hands; and the man shall give unto the woman a ring on this wise: the minister taking the ring shall deliver it unto the man, to put it upon the third finger of the woman's left hand. And the man holding the ring there, and taught by the minister, shall say:*

With this ring I thee wed: in the name of the Father, and of the Son, and of the Holy Ghost. Amen.

> *And before delivering the ring to the man, the minister may say as followeth.*

Bless, O Lord, this ring, that he who gives it and she who wears it may abide in thy peace, and continue in thy favor, unto their life's end; through Jesus Christ our Lord. Amen.

> *Then, the man leaving the ring upon the finger of the woman's left hand, the minister shall say:*

Let us pray.

> *Then shall the minister and the people,*
> *still standing, say the Lord's Prayer.*

Our Father, who art in heaven, Hallowed be thy name. Thy kingdom come. Thy will be done, on earth, as it is in heaven. Give us this day our daily bread. And forgive us our trespasses as we forgive those who trespass against us. And lead us not into temptation, but deliver us from evil. For thine is the kingdom, and the power, and the glory, for ever and ever. Amen.

> *Then shall the minister add:*

O eternal God, creator, and preserver of all mankind, giver of all spiritual grace, the author of everlasting life; send thy blessing upon these thy servants, this man and this woman, whom we bless in thy name; that they, living faithfully together, may surely perform and keep the vow and covenant betwixt them made (whereof this ring given and received is a token and pledge), and may ever remain in perfect love and peace together, and live according to thy laws; through Jesus Christ our Lord, Amen.

> *Then shall the minister join their right*
> *hands together and say:*

Those whom God hath joined together, let no man put asunder.

> *Then shall the minister speak unto the*
> *company.*

Forasmuch as —————— and ————— have consented together in holy wedlock, and have witnessed the same before God and this company, and thereto have given and pledged their troth, each to the other, and have declared the same by giving and receiving a ring, and by joining hands; I pronounce that they are man and wife, in the name of the Father, and of the Son, and of the Holy Ghost. Amen.

> *The man and wife kneeling, the minister*
> *shall add this blessing:*

God the Father, God the Son, God the Holy Ghost, bless, preserve, and keep you; the Lord mercifully with his favor look upon you, and fill you with all spiritual benediction and grace; that ye may so live together in this life, that in the world to come ye may have life everlasting. Amen.

14

Reception and Good-byes

The wedding's done! With all its solemnity and spiritual beauty, it has passed. Next comes the reception. So, "now is the time for all good men to come to the aid of the party," for a reception is a party. It can be a dinner party, a punch-and-cake type party, or any number of variations between these two extremes.

I prefer the punch-and-cake type party for a number of reasons, not the least of which is that wedding clothes were meant to be married in, not to eat dinner in. It is very nearly impossible for most brides to sit down at a banquet table, let alone eat, with all the bouffant crinolines and long, tightly tapered sleeves. Also, at a dinner party only a few guests really get to enjoy the company of the bridal party, since the bride's table is nearly always excluded to the young people in the wedding. The minister, the parents and other relatives sit at other tables, with friends or guests sitting still farther away. But at the stand-up, cake-and-punch reception the wedding party can mingle among the guests and entertain (briefly anyway) nearly everyone.

What Time the Reception?

One of the first questions to ask yourself about your reception plans is when it shall be. Among the multitude of meaningless phrases in the English language, one of the most meaningless is that which frequently appears on wedding invitations—reception immediately following.

Please do not use this phrase if you mean an hour after the ceremony or an hour and a half or two hours! It is not good manners to invite guests to an "immediately following" reception, have them ushered out after the ceremony, pew at a time (which automatically puts them in line for the reception), and *then* you and the wedding party spend an hour being photographed.

If you say "immediately following" on the invitation, make it immediately following. If you prefer not to forego the posing for several formal wedding pictures of the whole party, then simply list the time of the reception an hour or an hour and a half after the ceremony. This is at least being more fair to your guests. I do not know a single person who enjoys waiting in line for anything. We are a generation of impatient people. And these people, *your* guests, perhaps have already waited in line to sign *your* guest register.

If the guests know the reception will be more than an hour later than the wedding, they can at least get into their air-conditioned cars and drive around the block, or call home to see how the baby-sitter is doing, or journey to the post office to mail that letter that has been stuck above the sun visor for three days.

So make a time schedule. Talk with your minister to determine how long the wedding will last. Talk with your photographer to determine how long it will take to make the formal pictures you desire. Add fifteen minutes for nose-powdering, and decide whether yours is really an "immediately after" reception or an hour and a half later.

The Receiving Line

The first thing that happens at a wedding reception is receiving the guests. The bride's mother, who is hostess, stands first in line. Because most people are vain enough to think, "Everyone knows my name," this poses a real problem for the bride's mother. Therefore, it is the social duty of a guest to tell her his name, if he has even the slightest doubt that she does not know it or has forgotten it. Some brides engage an announcer to stand at the head of the reception line. Upon receiving the name of each guest, he then repeats it with undeniably clear enunciation to the mother of the bride: "Mrs. Hubert Claxton." Then she can, with poise, introduce Mrs. Claxton to the next person, and so on down the line, making the reception and introduction of guests run smoothly.

If there is no announcer, the bride's mother has no choice when she comes to a familiar unnamed face but to ask the name herself. This sometimes can be very embarrassing, especially should the guest turn out to be the woman down the block. (How very different she looks in that hat than when she's hanging out clothes!)

The bride's father may or may not stand next to the hostess. If he elects not to, then he must circulate among the guests and look joyous. Next comes the groom's mother and the groom's father (he is also optional in some areas). Then the all-important bride and groom, and next the maid of honor and the best man. Many etiquette authorities leave off the best man and add bridesmaids. But I feel pretty strongly about leaving off bridesmaids, and if you do, I'd like the best man standing next to the maid of honor, please. Otherwise, the maid of honor stands there alone ending the receiving line like a dangling participle.

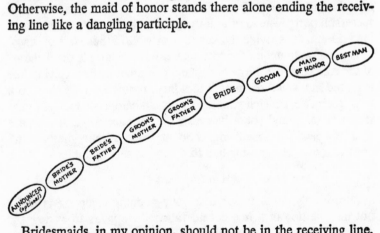

Bridesmaids, in my opinion, should not be in the receiving line. Guests run out of pretty adjectives and tire of hearing themselves echoing seven times, "It was a lovely wedding" or, "Your dress is so lovely." The bridesmaids tire of it, too. And they invariably forget what they are standing in a receiving line for—and that is, to introduce guests to the next in line. So, I think it far better to instruct the bridesmaids to make conversation with the guests—not just with each other and not just with the ushers!

One committee-minded young bride I remember chose a rainbow theme for her wedding. One bridesmaid was in pastel rose, one in pale green, one in lavender, and one in gold. She gave these specific and secret instructions to her bridesmaids to seek out the guests who were dressed in similar or neighboring shades on the color wheel and *entertain* them and their husbands. I'm sure that woman in the chartreuse and mauve striped dress wondered why nobody talked to her, but other than that, the plan worked beautifully. The bridesmaids *functioned*.

If you're not rainbow bent, you can think of other ways to mingle your bridesmaids. One can entertain all of the relatives from Sweet Springs and another the groom's aunt and uncle from Chicago. And you can assign an usher to tag along with each bridesmaid to help with the entertaining. There are lots of ways to make a reception a successful party instead of a drab, social obligation. And, functioning bridesmaids provide the key to nearly all of those lots-of-ways!

Another automatic door to a successful reception is the "where" of the receiving line. Flow of traffic is smoother if the receiving line is placed in a small room next to a large room, or at the door to a large room. So, squelch your urge to stand before the mantel in the family room. Stand yourselves near the entrance so guests can use all that space for socializing. And make sure your guests won't have to cross the receiving line to get to the serving tables.

What to Serve

Surprisingly, what to serve at your wedding reception is really not the question of prime consideration. Five years from now the guests won't remember whether it was *your* wedding cake that was baked from that special Parisian recipe or Susan Young's. The cake and punch should be tasteful, but if the fellowship is good and friendliness prevails, they can taste almost any old way, and people will invariably go away thinking that your reception was a big success. Why? Because, in your planning, you gave more attention to welcoming your guests and entertaining them than to the food to be served. Even when brides do give much attention to food details, it is *usually* not because they want to please their guests but that they want their wedding cake to be two tiers taller than Cathryn Long's and their punch gold to match their bridesmaids' gowns. A wedding cake has become a status symbol—for the bride, not for the guests. Guests have a sixth sense for detecting this. It is no wonder so many receptions are obligations rather than pleasures.

Lest you think I am not at all concerned about the delicacies you choose to serve, let me hasten to correct that impression. Here are some recipes that have successfully weathered many a reception punch bowl:

Golden Wedding Punch *

> 1 large can pineapple juice
> 1 6-oz. can frozen lemon juice
> 2 6-oz. cans frozen orange juice

Dilute frozen juices according to the instructions on the can. Add a cup or more of sugar—to your taste. And just before serving add a quart of Ginger Ale. Serves 25–30.

Wedding Punch

> 2 pkgs. raspberry Jell-O
> 1 cup hot water
> 7 cups cold water
> 1 large can pineapple juice
> Juice from
> 3 lemons and
> 6 oranges

Dissolve Jell-O in hot water. Add other ingredients. Make a syrup with 1 cup sugar (or more to taste) and ½ cup water. Just before serving add 1 large bottle of Ginger Ale. This punch is rosy-pink and will pour from 25 to 30 cups.

Parsonage Wedding Punch

1 quart water
½ cup (or more) granulated sugar
½ cup corn syrup
2 quarts strawberries
3 cups chilled orange juice
1 cup chilled lemon juice
1 quart Ginger Ale
2 thinly sliced limes

Combine first 3 ingredients. Bring to a boil; add the washed, stemmed, and sliced strawberries, and boil, covered, three minutes. Remove, strain through a sieve without pressing, and chill. Just before serving, combine with remaining ingredients. Leave in slices of strawberries if you want to serve with a flourish. Pours 25 to 30 cups.

Champagne for Your Reception?

For you critics who have been wading through these recipes eager to learn what I have to say about wedding wines, here it is. It won't take long to say it, for it is a strong opinion, supported by an equally strong conviction.

I *know* Jesus performed his first miracle in Cana of Galilee at a wedding feast. I am even aware that this miracle was the changing of water into wine. Jesus took water which was impure and by his very divinity transformed it into wine which was so good that it caused the steward (or master of ceremonies) of the wedding to exclaim: "Everybody I know puts his good wine on first and then when men have had plenty to drink, he brings out the poor stuff. But you have kept back your good wine till now!" (John 2:10).[1]

But I also *know* that when a Christian bride today seeks God's leadership in all of her wedding plans, she will not serve wine, or

---

* This recipe has the added advantage that you can file it away for your Golden Wedding celebration. Practically nobody will remember that it is the same punch!

[1] From *The New Testament in Modern English*, © J. B. Phillips, 1958. Used with permission of The Macmillan Company.

any kind of alcoholic beverage at her reception, even if it is held away from the church.

Does this mean that God has changed? I think not. To me it is only evidence of man's increasing debauchery, gluttony, and sinfulness. I have been led of the Holy Spirit to develop a conviction that a Christian today—to be an effective Christian—must practice complete, total abstinence from all alcoholic and fermented beverages.

Furthermore, even if I did not have this rigid conviction, I believe that there are holy moments in your life which should not be marred by liquor. One of these moments should be Christmas Eve, another, Christmas Day, and another, your wedding day. Make your wedding day a day of spiritual happiness and of complete sobriety. The Bible says:

> Live life, then, with a due sense of responsibility, not as men who do not know the meaning and purpose of life but as *those who do*. Make the best use of your time, despite all the difficulties of these days. Don't be vague, but firmly grasp what you know to be the will of God. Don't get your stimulus from wine (for there is always the danger of excessive drinking), but let the Spirit stimulate your souls. Express your joy in singing among yourselves psalms and hymns and spiritual songs, making music in your hearts for the ears of God! Thank God at all times for everything, in the name of our Lord Jesus Christ (Eph. 5:15–20).[2]

The Wedding Cake

You will want the traditional, white-tiered wedding cake. This tradition originated in Europe, where formerly it was customary to serve individual spice cakes at wedding receptions. These little cakes were put into a big mound over which the bride and groom were to kiss. If they managed this kiss without knocking any of the cakes down, they would live happily ever after. Somewhere along the way, a French cook conceived the idea of icing all those cakes together, so that fewer would be knocked off and more people would live happily ever after. Hence, the tiered wedding cake.

---

[2] From *The New Testament in Modern English*, op. cit.

Unless you have an aunt or grandmother who is a *never-fail* cake-maker and an artist at decorating, you'd better turn this responsibility over to a caterer or a professional baker. Do not try to have enough tiers to feed all of your guests. Have as many as you can afford and supplement them with sheet cake or petits fours.

A word to the wise, tier cakes look bigger and photograph nicer if the separate tiers are supported by decorative pillars. Ask your baker about this. It also makes the cake easier to cut.

The bride and groom together cut the first slice of cake. "When" to do this is a decision you will want to make early in your reception planning.

If yours is a rather small reception, the receiving line may be formed immediately after the wedding and all of the guests received before the bride and groom cut the cake. In this manner all of the guests may watch the cutting of the cake. But this does pose a few problems. The guests are left in a hanging state between the receiving line and the serving of refreshments. This is why it is so important to leave bridesmaids and ushers out of the receiving line and have them entertaining guests. A bridesmaid should have a three-minute alarm imprinted indelibly in her mind and should limit herself to conversation with each group to about that length of time—then on to the next group. This gives guests a feeling of participation rather than merely onlooking.

If you have a large wedding with many guests, there is no alternative. Most of them will be kept waiting (usually out of view), while you and the groom go through the cake-cutting ceremony in the presence of the wedding party, the families, and the photographer.

The bride holds the knife in her right hand. The groom places his hand over her hand, and together they cut the first slice from the bottom tier. Custom dictates that this slice be halved and that the bride feed the groom part and the groom feed the bride part—a sticky custom. In the interest of every bride who has ever been strangled by her husband's efforts to push a piece of sawdusty cake down an already parched throat, I suggest a sneaky alternative.

When the piece has been cut, place it on a serving plate, on which a reception assistant places a punch cup, nuts, and mints. Then declare sweetly, "I want my grandmother to have the honor of eating the first piece of my wedding cake."

Present it to her with a smile and a kiss and dash back to the receiving line.

Reception assistants, take note: No gesture in the world is quite

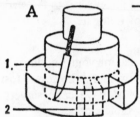

A

—Cut vertically through the bottom layer at the edge of the second layer as indicated by the dotted line marked 1; then cut out wedge-shaped pieces as shown by 2.

When these pieces have been served, follow the same procedure with the middle layer: cut vertically through the second layer at the edge of the top layer as indicated by dotted line 3; then cut out wedge-shaped pieces as shown by 4.

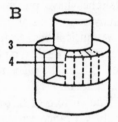

B

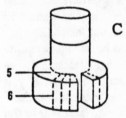

C

—When pieces from the second layer have been served, return to the bottom layer and cut along dotted line 5; cut another row of wedge-shaped pieces as shown by 6.

—The remaining tiers may be cut into the desired size pieces.

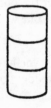

D

so thoughtful as that of the reception assistant who has ready for the bride and groom a glass of cold water for a quick refresher before starting to greet that long line of guests.

Some brides also wish to provide small pieces of boxed cake to send home with their guests to dream on. This cake, usually called "groom's cake," is frequently a dark fruitcake. The pieces are cut and wrapped well in advance. I have heard of a Sunday School class of women which takes this responsibility for the couples who marry in their church. They bake the cake, wrap and deliver it to the wedding ready to be distributed, and they enjoy doing it!

Minute Minders

Before you rent or buy serving accessories for your wedding reception, check with your church secretary or church hostess. Most churches have punch bowls and cups. Most have cake servers. Many own candelabra. Some provide long table cloths.

A musical background is a must for a beautiful reception, even if it is no more than a piano background of wedding music. Remember, here is the place to use that favorite song you couldn't use in the sanctuary.

The custom of throwing your bouquet originated in fourteenth-century France with the tossing of the bride's garter. Sometime down through the centuries, a modest bride, or one who wanted to keep both stockings up, elected to toss her bouquet instead.

One book I read suggested that the bride toss her bouquet picturesquely from a moonlit balcony or veranda to her bridesmaids below. This is fine if you happen to have a moonlit balcony. If you don't, the church entrance is the next best place, especially if there are steps. You simply give your bouquet an impartial toss into the air over the outstretched arms of your bridesmaids. Tradition says that the one who makes the lucky catch will be the next to the altar.

The Party's Over—It's Time to Call It a Day

After you have received all of the guests, cut the cake, and tossed your wedding bouquet, you are free to retire from the reception, if you wish, to dress for going away.

Nobody really expects you to be thoughtful at this point, so if you are, it *really* adds stars to your thoughtfulness crown.

When you are ready to leave, send for your parents—you have two sets of them now—so that you can tell them good-bye quietly, and so that you can again say "thank you"!

Consider these individual bits of thoughtfulness: One bride I know insisted on keeping on her bridal outfit so that she could go by her ailing grandmother's home and show her exactly how she looked at her wedding.

Another bride I know was distressed because she could not untangle her Bible from her bouquet. She asked to borrow a Bible to take on her honeymoon, so that she and her new husband could read God's Word every day.

Many couples call their parents as soon as they have reached their honeymoon hideaway.

Such gestures are the foundation of a happy married life. In the important area of getting along with each other, thoughtfulness is nearly as important as love itself. Thoughtfulness is love *expressed*.

And now, your wedding was practically perfect in every way!

Drive carefully!

And "may the Lord bless you, and keep you!"

Your Wedding Check List

First Things First

———Set the date.

———Visit the minister. Engage his services, establish the date of the wedding and the rehearsal date on the church calendar. Arrange for premarital counseling sessions.

———Decide on the type of wedding.
Informal
Semiformal
Formal

———Go into a huddle with your parents and work out the financial budget.

———Choose your attendants.

Maid of honor	Ushers
Best man	Guest book attendant
Bridesmaids	Organist
Flower girl	Soloist
Ring bearer	Other musicians
Pages	Reception assistants

———Decide where your reception will be held. Make arrangements for decorating in advance.

———Choose a florist, decide on wedding decorations, and tentatively order flowers.

———Shop for your wedding dress.

———Shop for attendants' gowns, taking maid of honor with you.

———Discuss style and color with attendants.

------Make your guest list. Secure list from groom's family and co-ordinate it with yours.

------Visit your stationer and order invitations and other stationery items you may need.

Next Things Next

------Address envelopes for the invitations. Your stationer will probably provide these in advance.

------Get somebody to be in charge of the reception. Hire a caterer, or accept the offer of the church hostess or Aunt May.

------Discuss costs of the reception with that someone. Set up a reception budget.

------Mail invitations (three weeks before wedding date).

------Choose a photographer.
Arrange to have formal portrait made.
Contract photographer's services for the wedding.

------Plan a trousseau tea—or plan to display your gifts at the reception. Make display arrangements.

------Write thank-you letters promptly as gifts arrive.

------Make appointment with your hairdresser.

------Wedding gown fittings:
Dates: ------------ ------------ ------------

------Pastoral counseling sessions:
Dates: ------------ ------------ ------------

------Showers:
Dates: ------------ ------------ ------------

------Other Parties—dates and places:
Trousseau tea: ------------ ------------
Bridesmaids' luncheon: ------------ ------------
Out-of-town guests ------------ ------------
Other: ------------ ------------

Last Things Last

------Wedding gown finished and ready to wear, hidden away in your closet.

------Do you know how many people have returned acceptances for the reception?

------Have you given this information to your caterer?

------Arrange to obtain the marriage license.

------Arrange for physical examinations.

------Make final arrangements for rehearsal and rehearsal dinner.

ALL SET?

———Guest book table.

———Cover for it.

———Candle or bud vase to decorate it.

———Guest book purchased.

———Pens available.

———Is the florist arranging for the canopy, the aisle cloth, the prie-dieu?

———What about tables at the reception?

———What about the ring bearer's pillow?

———The flower girl's basket?

———Is your going-away outfit all ready?

———Your luggage packed?

———Have you something old, something new, something borrowed, and something blue?

———And, have you prayed that God will add his blessing to your wedding? "In all thy ways acknowledge him, and he shall direct thy paths" (Prov. 3:6).